A WHISPER WILL BE HEARD

Philip Crowe

With a Foreword by the Archbishop of Canterbury

Fount
An Imprint of Harper Collins*Publishers*

Fount Paperbacks is an Imprint of
HarperCollins*Religious*
Part of HarperCollins*Publishers*
77–85 Fulham Palace Road,
Hammersmith, London W6 8JB

First published in Great Britain in 1994
by Fount Paperbacks
1 3 5 7 9 10 8 6 4 2

A catalogue record for this book
is available from the British Library

ISBN 0 00 627857-4

Typeset by Harper Phototypesetters Limited,
Northampton, England
Printed and bound in Great Britain by
HarperCollinsManufacturing Glasgow

For Freda
in deep gratitude for over thirty years
of partnership, friendship and love

To Elisabeth, Michael and Jamie
who live for a more just future

and in memory of my father
who was always true to his word
January 1904–April 1993

CONTENTS

FOREWORD

As any parent or teacher knows, the cry 'it's not fair' is common to every home and school. It may come as a call for just distribution of resources, be that the size of a piece of cake or the amount of pocket money; it may be a request for greater equality, whether of bedtime or television watching; it may well be a demand for what is perceived to be an inequitable punishment of another. Whichever it is, the appeal for 'fairness', for 'justice', is deeply rooted in each one of us.

But where does it come from? Does it make absolute demands? What are its implications for us as individuals, as communities, as nations and as part of the international order? It is questions like these that Philip Crowe seeks to address in *A Whisper Will Be Heard*. Using all his experience both as a pastor and as a theological teacher, he wrestles with some of the greatest challenges currently facing the human race. It is a book that refuses to opt for easy answers. It is designed to stimulate and provoke and will not therefore be agreed with by everyone. What it will do, I hope, is to provide a valuable resource for many individuals and parish groups as they seek to deepen their understanding of God – both of his justice and, still more importantly, of his righteousness.

1995 marks the fiftieth anniversary of the start of Christian Aid, so it is particularly appropriate that this book offers a significant and important exploration of what justice means in the contemporary world. I am grateful to Philip for writing this book and I pray that God will use it to deepen the faith of many.

+ George Cantuar

INTRODUCTION

The Cathedral Close in Salisbury has provided the setting and the inspiration for such varied works of literature as Trollope's Barsetshire Chronicles, William Golding's *The Spire*, and Susan Howatch's Starbridge novels. Writing a book about justice in an attic room high up in Salisbury and Wells Theological College, overlooking that same Close, has been an interesting experience. The whole area, not just the Close but the countryside for miles around, is dominated by Salisbury Cathedral, its slender spire pointing far into the heavens. It is a building of extraordinary beauty and power, which is able to refresh the human spirit and so make possible the dream and the hope of justice. Without such dreams, disillusionment and despair might quickly prevail. But other no less powerful influences have shaped this book apart from the beauty of the Cathedral and the glorious singing of its choir.

My wife and I spent February 1994 at the Tantur Institute, just outside Jerusalem, in order to find a different context in which to work; and we are grateful to the Tantur community, to the Trustees, and to the St Boniface Trust, for making that month possible. The army checkpoint which controls entry into the West Bank on the Jerusalem-Hebron road is near to the gates of Tantur, and we were woken most mornings by the call of the minarets in

Bethlehem, and by the noise of army loudspeakers and sirens.

Thirty-six hours before the massacre in Hebron, we were visiting a school in the town and experiencing at first hand the dreadful, almost palpable tension in the Tomb of the Patriarchs. Some of my writing, and a good deal of rewriting, was done not in the quiet of the Close, but close to the West Bank in Palestine, with the noise of shooting, explosions, and occasionally a deathly silence, all around.

The final revision of the manuscript was completed in a different silence, during a week spent at the Abbey on Iona, in the context of the rigour of Celtic Christianity and the concern of the Iona Community for peace and justice. But far more influential than either a week in Iona or a month in Palestine were the years spent in parochial ministry in the Church of England.

The six years which I spent on the staff of St Martin's-in-the-Bull Ring, in the centre of Birmingham, and eleven years as rector of the Derbyshire village of Breadsall, gave me differing perceptions of justice, and of the relation between justice and the Christian Gospel. The Archbishop of Canterbury's invitation to write this book for the series of study books he commissions each year has given me the opportunity to pursue the connections between the justice of God, the death of Christ and the life of the world.

My eighteen years in ordinary parish ministry also gave me a deep respect for the people who are the Church. R. H. Tawney said of the Church in the seventeenth century that 'The social teaching of the Church had ceased to count because the Church itself had ceased to think.' My experience in parish ministry is of people who are willing to engage with important questions of justice, and to think seriously and theologically about them, and I have tried to write a book which respects and honours such people.

For over twenty years, I have also enjoyed the difficult and rewarding task of contributing to the 'Today' programme on BBC Radio 4, and of responding to the large numbers of letters from an audience which can spot holes in an argument even while shaving, eating cornflakes, or rushing children to school. The discipline of relating Christian theology to immediate and contemporary events in a way which is supposed to be light and deep, provocative and reassuring, is a demanding and creative discipline, and I am glad of the opportunity to express my gratitude to many hundreds of correspondents, and to the BBC producers and presenters of the 'Today' programme, whose influence on my thinking is profound.

My writing has all been done during the final year of Salisbury and Wells Theological College, a year in which I and some of my colleagues have experienced the debilitating effects of being made redundant. The life of the college will continue for some time in the ministry of women and men now ordained; and to them and to all my colleagues on the staff, particularly to those who sustained the community with such style and vigour during its final year, I offer my deepest thanks: in particular to Fiona Torrance, College Secretary for eight years and my personal assistant for six, who has tranferred my scribblings onto a computer with the same unfailing good humour which has cheered generations of ordinands on their way; and to Janet Tomlinson, Tutor in Christian Doctrine, who has read the whole manuscript, parts of it a number of times, as if it were a dissertation submitted by a student, and has made innumerable comments ranging from tiny corrections to major points of Christian doctrine ('Now you know what it's like!', her other students tell me.) I am grateful for her thoroughness, perception, and rigorous encouragement.

The title is suggested in part by the Song of the Servant of the Lord in Isaiah chapter 42:

> Behold my servant whom I uphold,
> My chosen, in whom my soul delights;
> I have put my Spirit upon him,
> He will bring forth justice to the nations.
>
> He will not shout or lift up his voice,
> Or make it heard in the street.
> He will not fail or be discouraged
> Until he has established justice in the earth.

The phrase itself comes from a poem by a Jewish poet, Yehuda Amichai:

> In the place where we are right,
> Flowers will never bloom
> In the Spring.
> The place where we are right
> Is trodden and hard
> Like a courtyard.
> But like a mole, like a plough,
> Doubts and loves make
> The world crumble.
> And a whisper will be heard
> Where once there was a house
> That was destroyed.

Philip Crowe,
Holy Week and Easter, 1994.

ONE

EQUAL JUSTICE

'We'll keep one each for food,' the spokesperson announced, in a confident, almost defiant tone. 'We're going to keep one spare for snacks, crisps and things. We'll give one to Africa. And we're going to sell the other two to buy computers and weapons and cars.'

The children in the top class in the village school were thinking about the distribution of food. There were thirty-two children, aged nine to eleven. They were divided into six groups, to represent North America, South America, Europe, Africa, India and the Far East. Very roughly, the number of children in each group was in proportion to the actual population in those six parts of the world.

They were provided with forty bread rolls, representing the total world food production, one each and eight spare. Just as the children were divided between six areas of the world, to correspond to the actual population, so too the food was shared out very roughly in the way food is actually available. Africa, for example, had eight children and four rolls. Europe had six children and ten rolls.

The children sat in their six groups, each group round a table, looking at their bread rolls, and then quickly counting the number of rolls on each of the other tables. They had been presented with an allocation which they could see immediately was manifestly unfair. They were asked to decide what they wanted to do about it. Whether they realized it or not, they brought with them to the exercise the values and the prejudices they had acquired from their families, from television, from their school, and from elsewhere in their ten years of life. They also brought the accumulated likes and dislikes of their various classmates.

They spent a long time talking. The North American and European groups were still whispering long after the others had fallen into a resentful silence. The North American group had the most rolls but the children were English, not American, and what they decided did no credit to either the United States or Canada. Their decision is best left shrouded in diplomatic silence.

It was the European group which decided to keep one roll each for food, and one spare to share between them for snacks. They were determined and explicit in wanting to give one roll to Africa, not to the whole group representing Africa, but to one boy in particular because he was a friend of theirs. They felt sorry for him, that he had ended up in the African group and not with them. When the other African children protested that the roll should be given to all of them equally, a European boy grabbed the roll off his table, dashed across the room, put it into the hand of his African friend, glared defiantly at the other African children, and rushed back to Europe.

Other members of the European group, deciding also to leap into action, took their two spare rolls round the room and pretended to trade with them for computers, televisions, cars, and weapons. Asked why they needed weapons, one boy answered, almost casually, 'To make sure we keep what we've got'. Meanwhile a fight broke out, not between Africa and Europe but within Africa, because the boy who was friendly with Europe refused to share the roll he'd been given, and the others tried to grab it from him. The lesson degenerated into chaos, with a lot of shouting.

The bewildered teacher had embarked on the exercise naively expecting that nice children from good homes would quickly decide to share the rolls out equally. He bravely decided that the right thing to do educationally was to allow the noisy chaos to continue. It was abruptly ended by the head teacher, trying to work in the next room, who knew what was being attempted and was not as naive as the teacher. He rang the bell early for break.

ONE TOO LARGE, ONE TOO SMALL

'What is just,' wrote Aristotle in the fourth century BCE, 'is what is proportional, and what is unjust violates the proportion. So one share become too large and the other too small. This is exactly what happens in practice; the man who acts unjustly gets too much and the victim of injustice too little of what is good.'[1] Justice is the virtue which lies midway between two vices, either of seeking more or of obtaining less than one deserves. It is, suggests Aristotle, 'a sort of proportion'. He reaches that conclusion, not by playing games with bread rolls, but by a discussion which has defined the shape of people's thinking about justice for generations.

Just one page into a discussion on the promising question, 'What do we mean by justice and injustice?', Aristotle finds that the words are ambiguous. Despite the clarity of his subsequent discussion, the ambiguity persists in a modern dictionary which defines justice as 'the quality of being just'. Aristotle, like many people, finds it easier to begin by recognizing experiences of injustice, as either breaking the law, or taking advantage of another person, or both. 'Unjust', he says, 'means both unlawful and unfair. Just means lawful and fair. The unjust man takes more than his share.'[2]

He divides justice into two kinds, corrective justice and distributive justice. Being fined for speeding is an experience of corrective justice. So too is being imprisoned for committing murder, or for doing anything else which damages the just order of society. Distributive justice is an agreed and just principle by which the benefits of a society are distributed amongst its members. Whether men and women should have the same pension rights at the same age is a discussion about distributive justice. The contents of the Chancellor's battered case on Budget Day are concerned largely with questions of how much money society needs to spend, where it is come from, and who is to receive how much, all questions concerned with the distribution of resources.

Justice in the distribution of goods demands equality, Aristotle states. But he is less naive than the class teacher who assumed that nice children from good homes would share the forty rolls out equally. Justice may mean equal shares, argues Aristotle, but only if the people are equal. If they are not equal, they will not have equal shares. The shares, he says, must be in proportion to the persons. 'It is when equals are assigned unequal shares, or equal shares are given to people who are not equal, that complaints and quarrels break out.'[3]

When the children returned after break, and the dust had settled, they came to conclusions with which Aristotle might have agreed, though he would then have raised a great many other questions. No one wanted anyone else to starve. Some wanted everything to be shared equally. Most decided that equal shares would be unfair. They agreed that everyone should have a fair proportion, but not exactly the same amount each. How that fair proportion should be calculated was as problematic to the children as it had been to the Greek philosophers before them.

The simplest definition of justice, one of the oldest and most often quoted, is that justice consists in giving to every person what he or she deserves. Like most definitions, it merely pushes the question one stage further back. How are we to decide what a person deserves? If, for example, justice requires that equal people deserve equal shares, then equality requires most careful definition. The Equal Opportunities Commission once issued a circular which stated that 'If you are pregnant, and are dismissed from your job, you may be able to claim for unfair dismissal. We have to show that your employer would have treated a man differently in similar circumstances.' Aristotle's suggestion that justice must be based on 'some kind of equality' is vague and unsatisfactory. A clear answer to the question of whether human beings are equal, and in what sense, is fundamental to the pursuit of justice, and a substantial part of this first chapter will explore differing understandings of equality.

A BRIEF OUTLINE OF THE BOOK[4]

In certain basic matters, human beings are clearly equal; but it is the differences between people which makes human society interesting. The ideal of equal opportunities may be politically correct, but giving expression to that ideal without placing great restrictions on human freedom is immensely complex. The two views of equality which will be set out at the end of this first chapter reflect precisely the differences between the main political parties in Britain and America. One makes human needs primary, the other begins with human freedom. Carried to extremes, as they have been in recent history in different parts of the world, one view can produce a rigid Communist system, and the other can show the unacceptable face of Capitalism.

In the past, these different views have been measured by the standards of justice, a standard which has been set for most Western countries by the dominance of the Christian tradition. That tradition will be explored in the second chapter with particular reference to those two pivotal events, the binding of Isaac and the death of Christ, both, on the face of it, glaring acts of injustice. They raise the question of whether there is any absolute justice.

The third and fourth chapters will consider what the varying perceptions of justice may mean in practice for society and for individuals, and the final chapter will ask what kind of people we must be if we are ever to climb that mountain whose summit may be justice. But our exploration begins with the fundamental question of human equality.

STARK INEQUALITY

Playing games with bread rolls in order to learn about the unequal distribution of food is only possible in a society which has bread enough and to spare, for 'unequal distribution' is the polite way of talking about starvation and death. Forty bread rolls would be like manna in some villages. Prosperous countries whose success is based on the free market have yet to demonstrate that they can provide for the poor of the world. For while a great deal is done to relieve poverty and starvation, Western nations have also done great harm to poorer countries, and they continue to do so.

It is a notorious fact that most of the poorest countries are crippled by debt. Every day throughout the 1980s, the poorest countries were required to pay the richest countries over 17 million dollars in interest on loans. Each year now the poorest countries receive huge sums from the West in various forms of aid; in 1991, that sum was 137.2 billion dollars. People in the West sometimes feel good about being so charitable, sometimes resentful about being so generous. But in the same year, the poorest countries paid the West 151 billion dollars in interest on loans. The richest countries acquired from the poorest countries a surplus of 13.8 billion dollars, and good feelings of benevolence and charity to add to the bargain. If government grants and other forms of aid are left out of the account, and only charitable donations counted, then for every £1 individuals put into the collecting boxes of organizations like Christian Aid and Oxfam, the poorest nations pay back £9 in interest on loans.[5]

The exercise with bread rolls, which caused fighting amongst the children in the village school, was repeated some months later with a group of over sixty people in an affluent part of England. They were thinking about social justice and Third World debt. Most were middle-aged, reserved, cultured people. Instead of bread rolls they were given dog biscuits. The North American group consisted of eight people. They had fourteen dog biscuits.

After five minutes of dignified inaction, curious things began to happen. Some heated discussions and negotiations began. A man in his late sixties, dressed like a company executive, crawled across the room to reach under the chairs of the North American group and steal a dog biscuit from them. He was pounced on and forcibly stopped. Two women from Central Asia walked slowly back home from a visit to America. 'We have explained,' they said with great dignity, 'that we are from a fine country with a long and cultured civilization, and that we are in need. They have refused us.' 'They' were the relatively small North American group, which ended up sitting in a very tight circle. They had given dog biscuits away, traded carefully, and made some loans. They had started with fourteen. They ended with seventeen.

The global figure for Third World debt is a very long line of noughts: over 1,500,000,000,000 dollars. To a great many children in Zambia and other countries, that line of noughts means deprivation, hunger, and crushing poverty. The restructuring of national economies to service the debt means reductions in health care, education, and every kind of welfare provision. To the poor in many countries, those noughts add up to a slow death from starvation. The poor of the Third World are the reverse side of the wellbeing of the more fortunate nations, whose continuing good fortune they are made to serve.

There is a great deal of talk about reducing or even remitting part of the debt, but the sums involved are small, and little is actually done. Intuitively perhaps, without wanting to acknowledge it too clearly, Western nations know that it is necessary to make sure that the poor remain poor. In the short term, it is in the interests of industrialized nations to improve the economies of countries which are economically poor, so as to have an expanding market for consumer goods, thereby ensuring that economic growth is maintained. But in the long term, such expansion in developing countries would be disastrous. The consumption of commercial energy in India averages out at the equivalent of around 210 kilograms of oil per person each year. In Western countries, that figure is 3,765 kilograms per person per year.[6] If oil consumption in India were the same as that elsewhere, resources would be inadequate to maintain the Western way of life, while the damage done to the environment would be catastrophic. Does talk about human equality mean anything in a world of such stark inequality ?

EQUAL IN PHYSICAL NEED

'All men are created equal,' states the famous opening sentence of the American Declaration of Independence, and it maintains that this truth is 'self-evident'. But it is not self-evident. In America in 1776, when the Declaration was written, native Americans were dispossessed and black Africans sold as slaves. Such truth was far from self-evident. Thomas Jefferson's original draft for the Declaration begins differently. 'We hold these truths to be sacred and undeniable; that all men are created equal.' A sacred truth is not necessarily self-evident.

It is obvious, of course, that whether they wash in the river or in water which flows through gold taps, whether they eat gourmet food in an exclusive restaurant or scavenge for scraps in the dustbins outside, all human beings are equal in sharing the same basic physical needs. At the raw physical level, human beings and animals have much in common. But it would be absurd to conclude that because they share the same physical needs, human beings and animals are equal.

It is not even clear from observation of the natural order that people are equal; indeed the most casual observation of human beings leads to the conclusion that they are far from being equal. They are unequal in physique, in beauty, in intelligence, in artistic ability, in perception, in application, in almost every conceivable way. Nor is it apparent that a person's lack of ability in one field will be balanced by great skill in another; for some people can do almost anything with a simple excellence while others lack even the most basic natural ability.

Our growing knowledge of genetics tells that the source of this inequality is not simply human greed, but that it is built in to the natural order. 'It is a profound truth,' said Sir Peter Medawar in the 1959 Reith Lectures, 'realized in the nineteenth century by only a handful of biologists and by philosophers hardly at all, that nature does not always know best; that genetical evolution, if we choose to look at it liverishly instead of with fatuous good humour, is a story of waste, makeshift, compromise and blunder.'[7]

The natural order is consistently random. Ability and disability are distributed without reference to race, gender, wealth or position. But if justice consists in rendering to every person impartially what he or she deserves, then nature may be impartial, but nature is also unjust. Does one person deserve to be born with a crippling hereditary disease, while the majority are born healthy? Long life and early death, sickness and disease, are distributed with an impartiality which serves the purposes of the natural order, but which has scant regard for any of the other, most basic principles of justice.

It is not even clear from the natural order that life itself is sacred. Animals and insects are not all vegetarians. Charles Darwin had a famous problem with a peculiarly nasty kind of parasitic wasp, which paralysed caterpillars, and stored them as living food for its larvae. 'I cannot persuade myself', he wrote, 'that a beneficent and omnipotent God would have designedly created the Ichneumonidae (these parasitic wasps) with the express intention of their feeding within the living bodies of caterpillars.'[8]

Observation of the natural world turns out to be a

precarious basis for an understanding of human equality, since serious inequality, one species feeding off another, is an integral part of that world; which is uncomfortably similar to the reality of much of human behaviour. Yet the Roman Catholic Church bases a significant understanding of equality on what is generally called natural justice. It is rooted in the belief that every person has equal worth and dignity because in the natural order all are created equal.

This understanding of natural justice requires that goods and resources should be shared fairly, on the basis of need, rather than desert. Ownership is for the benefit of all, and all means not just my family or my country, but embraces all people. What is surplus must be measured not by my own estimate of my reasonable needs, but by the needs of others and by the total available resources.[9]

Even so brief an account of this understanding of social justice indicates how revolutionary it is. But though it is said to be derived from observation of the natural world, it is not based on natural justice alone. The Greek philosophers made great use of this kind of thinking, but they were writing before the Christian era, and they did not come to conclusions like these. What is often described as natural justice is more often the natural world seen in the light of Christian revelation. The bald statement that all are created equal derives its power from the belief that every human being is created in the image and likeness of God.

EQUAL AS MORAL PERSONS

Even the most careful observation of the natural word tells us little beyond the fact that human beings are equal in their need for the basic requirements of life. Does human reason get us any further? There is a long tradition which runs from Plato and Aristotle through the Enlightenment to philosophers such as Immanuel Kant in the eighteenth century and John Rawls in the 1970s, which holds that human beings can work out what is just and unjust by rational argument.

Plato, writing three hundred years before the death of Christ, developed the idea of ultimate reality as the truth behind the appearance. An analogy concerning dogs is not likely to have appealed to him – Plato probably preferred horses to dogs – but think of the judge who has the unenviable task of choosing the supreme champion at Crufts. For years, she has studied dogs, lived with them, talked about them, handled them, judged them. When she looks at the champions of the various breeds, she carries with her, as part of her very being, the idea of the perfect dog, the dog she has not yet ever seen, perhaps never will.

The ideal exists not just in her mind, but in her feelings and even in her fingertips. It is part of her. It is her perception of the perfect idea of what a dog is. But that ideal is not created by her own subjective experience. The ideal exists, independent of her, in the breed standards, which represent the best attempt to decide what the perfect dog would be like. The standard by which the supreme champion is judged is that particular judge's perception of the ideal.

Plato, had he used this analogy, would have maintained that the perfect dog is the ultimate reality, and every particular living dog is an appearance of it. He argues that beauty, truth and goodness exist prior to and independently of all our thinking about them. Justice is more than an ideal which exists in our heads, or which is derived from our experience. It is not just a matter of personal opinion or subjective feeling or cultural prejudice. The general ideal of justice is the true reality. It is that objective ideal which gives value and meaning to the particular expressions of justice in human society. It is by that ideal that all our human attempts at justice are to be judged.

Over the years, the standard by which dogs have been judged has changed, sometimes quite dramatically. There have been periods when fashion has dictated curious and sometimes highly disagreeable standards, as a result of which dogs have not merely suffered such discomforts as the docking of tails. They have been so carefully and selectively inbred as to become virtually dysfunctional as dogs. Plato's understanding of the idea and the appearance, taken seriously, might have provided some protection against these fashionable and undesirable trends. It would have required people to look upwards towards the ideal, and downwards towards the earthly appearance, and to judge the one by the best perception of the other.

Aristotle, following Plato, studied the 'appearances' of justice in the various societies which functioned, more or less successfully, in his own time. Like a travel guide he toured the cities of his day, observing and recommending those he considered well-ordered. 'Everyone agrees', he writes confidently, 'that justice in distribution must be in accordance with merit in some sense, but they do not all mean the same kind of merit: the democratic view is that the criterion is free birth; the oligarchic that it is wealth or good family; the aristocratic that it is excellence.'[10]

VIRTUE AS THE PURSUIT OF EXCELLENCE

What matters to Plato and Aristotle, and to other Greek thinkers, is excellence. Virtue is the highest good of human beings. The best kind of society is one in which the best people rule, and in which virtue is rewarded. But certain kinds of work, particularly a 'mechanical or commercial life'[11], and also farming, because it left no free time, were thought to militate against virtue. (Thomas Jefferson, by contrast, thought farming particularly conducive to a life of virtue; while banking, politics, and selling used cars might be the modern equivalents on Aristotle's black list.) He maintained that people engaged in such occupations should not be allowed the rights of full and equal citizenship. Nor should women, because, in Aristotle's view, possibly in his experience, they could not exercise the necessary control over their emotions. Nor slaves.

It is, he maintains, nature's intention that there should be physical differences between master and slave, the slave having the strength for manual labour, the master the more upright figure, and a body useless for hard labour, but ideally suited to the duties of civic life. By nature, claims Aristotle, the slave is different from his master. Destitute of reason, devoid of moral sense, a slave can neither think for himself nor make moral decisions. 'The slave is a living tool in the same way that a tool is an inanimate slave.'[12] Human beings are not equal, and for those with good muscles and no moral sense, 'the condition of slavery is both beneficial and just'.

Even before the birth of Christ, Aristotle had his critics. 'Under the civil law' wrote the Roman lawyer Ulpian, in the third century BC, 'slaves are reckoned as non-persons, but as far as the natural law is concerned, all men are equal.'[13]

The Stoics in the same period believed that all human beings are created with moral sense, and are therefore equal. 'Within us,' writes Seneca, 'a holy spirit has its seat, our watcher and guardian in evil and in good.' All are equal, because, in Virgil's phrase, in every human being 'there dwells nameless, dimly seen, a god'.

In fairness to Aristotle, he might have reached different conclusions had his powerful intellect been applied to contemporary society. Women in his day were largely deprived of education, and were still expected to meet high expectations and to fulfil the demands of incompatible roles. In such circumstances, occasional, or even frequent, outbursts of emotion, would be understandable; though not, apparently, excusable.

Aristotle and other Greek thinkers may have been ambivalent about human equality; John Rawls is crystal-clear. Rawls is typical of that tradition in philosophical thinking which uses reasoned argument without reference to religion. In 1972, when his book *A Theory of Justice* was published, John Rawls was Professor of Philosophy at Harvard University. His argument is developed without reference to God, and neither religion, church, Christian faith or God get a mention in the index. His starting point is what we share in common as human beings, in particular, 'our intuitive conviction of the primacy of justice'.[14] His long discussion and argument then tests the truth of this intuition.

Rawls suggests that human beings are equal, and deserve equal treatment, because all human beings are moral persons. 'There is', he says, 'no race or recognized group of human beings that lacks this attribute.' All human beings, are, without exception, moral persons.

Two essential features distinguish moral persons: 'They

are capable of having a conception of their good; and they are capable of having a sense of justice.'[15] These distinguishing features may be latent, as in children, a potential which is ordinarily realized in due course. They may therefore be stunted by impoverished social conditions, deformed by the undermining of self-worth, or corrupted through the influence of low moral standards. The children of criminals may develop a twisted conception of their good and a distorted sense of justice; but only because the capacity for good and for justice is corrupted, not because it is absent altogether. If people behave in such evil ways that their capacity for good and their sense of justice seem to be missing altogether, they are usually described as 'inhuman'.

EQUAL IN FAITH

People who believe in God may recognize this capacity for moral personality as one aspect of 'the image of God', in which women and men are created. The creation myths in the book of Genesis set the Tree of the Knowledge of Good and Evil in the centre of the garden. With great depth and subtlety, they tell that the knowledge of good and evil, and the freedom to choose between them, is both the glory and the burden of humanity. It is this capacity for moral personality which is unique to human beings, in which so much of the worth and dignity of every human being is focused, in which every person is equal, and therefore is entitled to equal justice.

The great creation myths and the reasoned arguments of the philosophers complement each other in reaching this conclusion; but Christian faith goes further than rational argument and holds to the belief that human beings are equal at the most fundamental level because every human being is equally loved by God.

Christians who observe the season of Lent can, if they choose, make an extraordinary journey. In modern Israel, in the north of Galilee, there is a place called Banias, where the headsprings of the River Jordan well up into lovely clear pools. It is today a National Park, with picnic tables among the trees. Somewhere in that region Jesus took his disciples, at the watershed of his ministry.

For months, he had been proclaiming the kingdom throughout Galilee. Then, one day, he began to walk away to the north of Galilee, gradually leaving the crowds behind. In the quiet countryside somewhere near Banias, then called Caesarea Philippi, he slowly leads his disciples towards the question – 'Who do you say that I am?' Peter's famous response, 'You are the Christ', marks the turning point in Jesus' life. 'From that moment he began to teach his disciples that the Son of Man must suffer.'[16] The last journey begins. Jesus takes his disciples to the Mount of the Transfiguration.

From that mountaintop he walks down through Galilee, again teaching the disciples about his suffering and death. Their journey skirts the hostile territory of Samaria, following the well-worn pilgrim tracks along the Jordan Valley for part of the way, and then they make the long, slow climb up the hills that are round about Jerusalem. When the city is in sight, Jesus stops. The disciples hang back, dreading something which they feel but do not begin to understand. Again Jesus tells them what will happen in Jerusalem. Again they fail to understand.

To travel with Christ from the Mount of Transfiguration to the Place of a Skull is to journey into the most extraordinary belief in all religion. Nothing could have prepared the disciples for what would happen at the end of that journey, still less for what it might mean. Only afterwards did they come to believe that the man with whom they had talked and laughed and walked is 'the image of the invisible God, by whom everything that exists was created'; that the man whose terrible death they had witnessed is the one 'in whom all things hold together'.

If it is true that God was in Christ, then everything in heaven and on earth is involved in that death. 'Christ died for all' means precisely that. All who lived before Christ, and all who have lived since, are part of his death, because the arms which were stretched out on the Cross are the arms that hold the entire universe in being. 'The crucified Jesus is the only accurate picture of God the world has ever seen,' writes John Baker, 'and the hands that hold us in existence are pierced with unimaginable nails.'[17]

In this death, in the love which caused it and the life which flows from it, every human being is equal. The determined, severe, self-giving love which moved Jesus on his final journey is the same love with which God loves every human being. The Cross shows us what God is always like. The life which flows from the Cross is offered equally to every person on precisely the same terms. It cannot be bought or earned. It is given freely, and has only to be received.

Gradually, in human society, sometimes painfully, and only after long and bitter struggle, a firm belief in the full equality of every human being has gained ground. The early church, though it saw no reason to question let alone abolish the institution of slavery, held firmly to the belief that every human being is equal in the sight of God. How could it do otherwise when it followed a man who treated every person he met with equal love, equal understanding, equal severity, equal compassion?

The reading Jesus chose when he spoke in the synagogue at Nazareth proclaims liberty for the captives, deliverance for the oppressed, and the judgement of God on all human institutions which undermine the dignity and worth of human beings. But nearly 400 years were to pass before anyone publicly advocated the abolition of slavery, partly because slavery was considered insignificant in comparison with the final end of the world order, an end which was expected to occur almost immediately.

'WHO CAN BUY A MAN?'

Late in the fourth century, as such hopes faded, Gregory of Nyssa wrote a homily on the book of Ecclesiastes. It is little known even among scholars, and has only recently been translated into English. He argues powerfully that the great worth and dignity of every human being demands the total abolition of slavery.

The writer of Ecclesiastes, seeking a life of pleasure through the acquisition of such consumer durables as were available in his day, includes among his purchases 'slaves and slave girls'. 'Tell me,' demands Gregory, 'what price did you pay for them? What did you find among your possessions that you could trade for human beings? What price did you put on reason? How many obols did you pay as a fair price for the image of God? For how many staters have you sold the nature specially formed by God? God said, "Let us make human beings in our image and likeness." Tell me this: who can buy a man, who can sell him, when he is made in the likeness of God?'[18]

In his time, Gregory stands alone, so far as our knowledge goes, in making connections between the worth and dignity of every human being and the need to give expression to that belief by abolishing an institution now recognized almost universally as a great evil. But it is surely no accident that the prime mover in the eventual abolition of the slave trade, William Wilberforce, was a Christian moved by the simple evangelical truth that 'Christ died for me', and if 'for me', then equally for every other human being.[19]

The abolition of slavery, the right to vote, equal rights for women, are all expressions in various societies of the recognition that every human being is of equal worth and dignity. That belief may be derived from some understandings of natural law; though not necessarily. It may be the result of a careful process of human reasoning; though there may be dispute over the meaning of that equality. But a firm belief in the equal worth and dignity of every human being arises directly out of the life, and particularly the death, of Jesus Christ.

Whether it is derived from belief in the Gospel and from faith in the God in whose image human beings are created, or from rational arguments that all people are equal as moral persons, or from an understanding of natural law, or from a combination of all three, the belief that every human being is of equal dignity and worth is the basic premise for all contemporary understanding of human rights. And it is the denial of that human equality which is one of the root causes of injustice. Both history and contemporary society are littered with examples.

ROOT CAUSE OF INJUSTICE

The Europeans who settled in South Africa after 1652 considered themselves superior in every way to the indigenous peoples, and rapidly established clear distinctions between Christian and heathen, white and black, civilized and uncivilized. In 1803, white colonists resisted the suggestion that native people be given equal protection in law on the grounds that they were heathen and therefore not truly human.

The great trek of the 1830s was caused in large part by Ordinance 50 of 1828 which was intended to make natives equal before the law, an ordinance which Afrikaners rejected as being 'in conflict with the laws of God and with natural distinctions of origin and belief'.[20] Out of such poisoned roots came the ugly growth of apartheid.

Notions of racial superiority were, and still are, fuelled by twisted interpretations of the Old Testament. Afrikaners saw themselves as 'the chosen ones', forbidden to mix with the native people who were considered equivalent to the Canaanites, the sons of Ham. The slave traders took a similar view. Black people were created inferior, ordained by God to be slaves. Sadly, it is characteristic of those who are abused that they come to accept the low opinion that others have of them. In the 1930s, a black child brought up in America's Deep South was deeply infected by this.

Legend tells that in the small town of Stamps, Arkansas, white people were so prejudiced against blacks that they would allow Negroes to buy vanilla ice cream on only one day of the year, American Independence Day. 'Of course,' writes Maya Angelou, whose childhood was spent in Stamps, 'I knew God was white too, but no-one could have made me believe he was prejudiced.'

She recalls the store where she grew up, crowded one night with black people listening to the radio. Joe Louis, heavyweight boxing champion of the world, was fighting another contender, this time a white man.

' "He's got Louis against the ropes," the commentator yelled, "the contender keeps raining the blows, it looks like Louis is going down." Men leaned towards the radio. My race groaned. It was our people falling. It was another lynching. If Joe lost we were back in slavery and beyond help. It would all be true, the accusation that we were lower types of human beings. Only a little higher than the apes. True that we were stupid and ugly and lazy and dirty and, unlucky and worst of all, that God himself hated us and ordained us to be hewers of wood and drawers of water, for ever and ever, world without end. We didn't breathe. We didn't hope. We waited.'[21]

Marwa Jibara grew up in Israel/Palestine in the 1970s. When she was eight, her Arab teacher told the class ('I still hate her for this,' says Marwa): 'Tomorrow we will celebrate our Independence Day, when the Jews came and liberated our land from the British.' Marwa asked her aunt to bake a cake for the party. 'The next morning I took the cake, such a pretty cake, and I was about to leave the house, when Father came and smashed and pulverized the cake with his fingers. I cried. I took it to school crying, and I told them that my father had done it, and I didn't know why. I was so naive.' She knows now.[22]

Today, Marwa Jibara is a leader of the Palestinian women's movement in Israel. David Grossman, who records her experience in his book of conversations with Palestinians in Israel, found himself reflecting, as he talked with her, of her father charging at her when she was a little girl, 'pulverizing her cake without a word. How violent that deed was, mixing political protest, male aggression, and humiliation of her young womanhood, now so contained, so clench-fisted.'[23]

That conversation evoked potent memories for Grossman of his own childhood: at the age of eight or nine, reading, understanding and not understanding, who is a Gentile, what is a pogrom, what is exile; reading the story of Tevye the milkman, not with the glamorous overlaying and catchy tunes of *Fiddler on the Roof*, but the raw words with their echoes of his own father's experience; finding himself, as he finished the story, sitting on the cart, in his fresh and vivid imagination, with Tevye and his daughter and his wife when they were driven out of Anatevka, and then realizing suddenly, inside, with a wail that shook him through and through, how hard it is to be a Jew, and simultaneously, for the first time, knowing that 'I am a Jew'.[24]

THE RIGHT LOOK IN THE EYE

Whether its victims are black or white, Arab or Jewish, the roots of injustice lie in the refusal to recognize the equal worth and value of other human beings. Arguments in favour of human equality, whether derived from natural law, reason, or religious experience, and theories of justice based upon such arguments, may be more or less persuasive. But even the best and most convincing of arguments will be of little use unless the truth of them is deeply felt.

'There you are, sir,' wrote the humanist Walter Lippmann in 1927, 'and there is your neighbour. You are better born than he, you are richer, you are stronger, you are handsomer, nay you are better, kinder, wiser, more likeable; you have given more to your fellow men and taken less than he, and yet – absurd as it sounds – these differences do not matter, for the best part of him is untouchable, and incomparable and unique and universal. Either you feel this or you do not: when you do not feel it, the superiorities that the world acknowledges seem like mountainous waves at sea; when you do feel it, they are slight impermanent ripples upon a vast ocean.'[25]

Society may be organized in accordance with strict principles of justice and fairness; but if people do not feel that they belong to one another, if they do not respect one another as equals, then even the best ordered society will be deeply corrosive of the human spirit.

There is a famous passage in the writings of Laurens van der Post. When the Dutch Empire in Indonesia was crumbling, the Governor General said to him: 'I cannot understand it. Look what we have done for them. Look at the schools and the hospitals we have given them. We have given them a prosperous, balanced economy. Everyone has enough to eat. We have given them an honest and efficient administration and abolished civil war and piracy. And yet they want us to go. Can you tell me why?' Laurens van der Post replied, 'Yes, I think I can: I'm afraid it is because you've never had the right look in the eye when you spoke to them.'

'It may sound inadequate,' he adds, 'but just think, for one moment, of the light that is in the eye of a human being when he looks at another human being he loves and respects as an equal. Then remember the look in the eye of the average European when he is in contact with a "lesser breed without the law", and you will understand what I mean.'[26]

It is however possible for two people to look each other

in the eye, to respect one another as equals, and yet disagree fundamentally on what equality means in practice.

TWO VIEWS OF EQUALITY

Two differing understandings of what human equality means are widely held in both British and American society. They underlie competing political systems, they inform people's decisions about which way to vote in elections, and they have been the cause of intense debate in moral philosophy since the early 1970s.

One view, which we have already considered, holds that human beings are all of equal worth and value. They may have differing abilities, but these are gifts distributed at random in the natural order. At the most fundamental level, the needs of human beings are equal. All need equal liberty and equal opportunity to achieve their full potential.

The other view holds that human beings are equal in their freedom to enjoy whatever they have achieved, to keep whatever they have acquired through legitimate means, and to use it in whatever way they choose. Human beings may have enjoyed equality of opportunity in some imaginary and idealized state, but it is in the nature of human beings that some make use of the opportunity they have, others do not. That too belongs to the equal and inviolable freedom of every individual.

These two views may be heard, in various forms, on the campaign trails in Britain and America whenever election time comes round. Those who are in need will argue for a redistribution of wealth and power in society, and their arguments will be supported by others who are not themselves in need, but who are convinced that justice demands such redistribution. Those who have struggled hard to buy their own house, to bring up their children, and to save for their old age, will resent having their hard-won and modest prosperity threatened by increased taxation, which is only intended, in their view, to provide hand-outs for those who live off the state.

Deliberately these arguments are presented in a way which is quickly degenerating into caricature. Much more could be said about the justice and injustice of these competing claims to equality, and more will need to be said later. The point here is that both views are held with great force and sincerity, both are based largely on reasoned argument, and both underlie differing political systems. Both have been expressed with great clarity by two different writers, Robert Nozick and John Rawls.

Their views have been given added significance because these two writers have been put into the ring together in a significant book called *After Virtue*, by Alasdair MacIntyre, where they are turned into the champions of their respective political corners – Rawls in the red corner and Nozick in the blue corner. Rawls argues for equality based on need, Nozick for equality based on the inviolability of the freedom of the individual.

MacIntyre uses this debate to make two substantial points: first, that Nozick and Rawls both hold a view of society which is wholly typical of – indeed it is largely formed by – the late nineteenth and twentieth centuries. It is the view that society consists of atomized individuals who each have their own view, and are each entitled to their own view, about the terms on which they will share in the life of society.

Secondly, MacIntyre sees no way in which the views of these two philosophers can be reconciled. To him this is evidence of the fact that attempts to provide a coherent moral or political philosophy, based on reason alone, all fail. They fail because those thinkers who make such attempts come up with as many different ideas as there are philosophers.

The fact that they disagree is not, as MacIntyre himself recognizes, decisive proof that their attempts fail. It is only a pointer in that direction. But it does inevitably mean that the discussions can run and run, inconclusively. Those arguments reflect precisely the views of traditional Labour and Conservative voters. 'It follows', writes MacIntyre, 'that our society cannot hope to achieve moral consensus. Modern politics is civil war carried on by other means.'[27]

THE END OF THE AGE OF ENLIGHTENMENT

MacIntyre has, of course, his critics, though a great many people find his arguments persuasive. They resonate with that intense frustration, felt by so many people, at the sterility of political debate in Britain and America. They echo the fears and the uncertainties of people in a society which is changing rapidly, and which keeps chipping away, nervously, at the base on which its lingering moral convictions stand.

The ideal of the Age of Enlightenment, which has so dominated European thought since the late seventeenth and eighteenth centuries, was that human beings would stand up for themselves, no longer at the mercy of uncontrollable nature, unpredictable force, or authoritarian dogma. Human beings would have the courage to use their own reason, to reject religious authority, and to discover a rational morality based on a scientific understanding of human nature.

For the writer, François Mauriac, the Age of Enlightenment ended suddenly and decisively, on a station platform. Trainloads of Jewish children, torn from their mothers, were standing at Austerlitz station. At that stage he did not know, could not imagine, the horrors that awaited them at the end of their journey; but the plight of those children was such a revelation of 'the mystery of iniquity that it marked the end of one era and the beginning of another. The dream which Western man conceived in the eighteenth century, whose dawn he thought he saw in 1789, and which, until 2 August, 1914, had grown stronger with the progress of Enlightenment and the discoveries of science – this dream vanished finally for me before those trainloads of little children.'[28]

Yet the legacy of the Enlightenment remains a powerful and ambiguous influence: on the one hand, a greater respect for human dignity, a rejection of authoritarian power, and a high regard for science and for human reason; on the other, a perilous moral uncertainty which increases as scientific knowledge and technology advance.

Natural law and scientific knowledge, together with human reason, do contribute significant and important insights to our understanding of human equality, and to the patterns of justice in contemporary society. But all have their serious limitations. All fail to provide absolute moral laws which are valid in all circumstances. They do not even provide an adequate basis for an objective morality, or for a general moral consensus.

Behind this exploration lies an issue which has assumed great importance for our society. When James Bulger, the toddler from Liverpool, was killed, and two ten-year-old boys were convicted of his murder, the whole nation was plunged into a period of questioning and self-doubt unparalleled in British society. Some years ago William Golding's book *The Lord of the Flies*, made us vividly aware of the fact that this kind of thing is possible; but that knowledge seemed to make little difference.

The death of that small boy touched a raw nerve. The most widely expressed fear was that people no longer know the difference between right and wrong. In spite of, or possibly because of, the fact that it is so rare an occurrence, the horrific murder of a small child by other young children was taken as a sign that 'mere anarchy is loosed upon the world'.

The need for shared moral values in society has been a consistent theme in the ministry of the present Archbishop of Canterbury ever since he came into office. In the introduction to a collection of his addresses and sermons, Bishop Richard Holloway writes that 'the danger, in pluralistic societies like modern Britain, where a variety of views are tolerated, is that society itself ends up with no set of common values or moral purposes. The Archbishop affirms many of the values of modern plural societies, but he is constantly pleading for the recovery of a common moral vision in our country . . . which affirms the value of personal freedom, and also acknowledges the need for a core of objective values and standards.'[29]

IS ABSOLUTE JUSTICE MYTH OR POSSIBILITY?

Does absolute justice exist? Is it ever possible to say, 'You must do this because it is absolutely right'; or 'You must never do this because it is always absolutely wrong, whatever the circumstances'? If the answer is yes, then absolute justice constitutes one part of what is sometimes called 'objective morality'. That somewhat clinical phrase indicates a morality that is not influenced by personal feelings or individual circumstances. It is 'out there', given, carrying with it authority of some kind. It tells people what to do, and when circumstances are extraordinarily bleak or unusually complex, knowing the right thing to do can be a great relief.

David was nearly seven when his mother realized, to her great dismay, that she was pregnant for a third time. Her second son, born when David was three, had been grievously handicapped. After four wretched weeks, he had died. His parents decided together not to have any more children. So this third pregnancy, confirmed at eight weeks, was not merely unwanted. It brought despair and horror, and the terrible fear that they would go through all that misery again.

One morning, the mother rang a clinic and through her tears, explained what had happened. The clinic told her to come in three days later, at 11.00 am. They would then terminate the pregnancy. No counselling was offered, nor was there any serious discussion. She told her story, the clinic accepted it, a decision was made.

Suddenly, to their immense relief, the parents were no longer trapped. They did not have to continue with the pregnancy. A way out had been offered. They were free to choose, to ask themselves whether they really wanted to end the pregnancy. After two days of intense discussion with a range of people, the mother rang the clinic again and cancelled the appointment.

Twenty-one weeks into the pregnancy, after all the tests had been made, the available evidence indicated a normal, healthy baby. David carried around a photograph of shadows and whirls taken from one of the scans, and excitedly pointed out to his puzzled school friends the outline of his baby sister. She was born safely and normally. Today she is at primary school.

It is quite rare, in circumstances such as these, for an abortion not to be carried out. It has been estimated that in the twenty years following the passing of the 1967 Act, three million abortions were carried out. In America, even more than in Britain, the abortion issue arouses most intense and bitter controversy. Both sides lay claim to absolute justice. One side seeks justice for the mother in the form of freedom of choice, the other demands justice for the unborn child, in the form of total protection. It is a rare but happy situation where giving the parents complete freedom of choice results in continuing life for the child.

For some people, opposition to abortion is a simple matter of natural justice. From conception onwards, they argue, a human being exists, genetically complete. Never mind the endless and inconclusive discussions about Who is a person? or When does personal life begin? At conception, a natural process is started which is continuous, and which ends naturally in the birth of a child. That child has a right to life. It is a matter of natural justice. Abortion is always and invariably wrong. The only circumstance in which the life of the fetus might be ended would be an operation to save the life of the mother.

For others, the right to freedom of choice, whether to have an abortion or not, is the woman's absolute right. It is an expression of that inalienable right to liberty which is considered essential to genuinely human life. When the Supreme Court in the United States made a decision limiting the right to abortion, the French health minister, Claud Evin, condemned the decision, and declared that 'women have an inviolable right to free choice over pregnancy'.[30]

These two rival views of absolute justice are precisely parallel to the contradictory understandings of equality, and of justice in society, which are set out by Rawls and Nozick. But is MacIntyre right when he says that 'we have all too many rival and disparate concepts of justice, and the moral resources of the culture allow us no way of settling the issue between them rationally'? Is it true that 'our society cannot hope to achieve moral consensus'?

TWO

WILL THE JUDGE OF ALL THE EARTH DO RIGHT?

Two different approaches to questions of morality and authority are now characteristic of all religions. They are polarized by the age of uncertainty in which we live, and by the lack of any clear moral consensus. On the one hand, there are those who long for familiar certainties, for basics in morality, a longing which is met by the rapid growth in all forms of religious fundamentalism.

On the other hand, there are people who recognize that complex modern questions cannot be answered by pious or dogmatic pronouncements without making religious experience look ridiculously naive at best, and destructive of human dignity and personality at worst. To replace uncertainty by religious tyranny only makes a bad situation worse, while to add religious questions to every other form of uncertainty only makes confusion intolerable. Both attitudes are apparent in the use that is made of the source books of religion.

Whether it is Muslims chanting the Qur'an, Jews reading Torah, or Christians studying the Bible, views about the authority and the accuracy of these sacred texts differ within all three religions. At one extreme within Christian faith, there is the view held by an Irish evangelist who visited Cambridge University when Michael Ramsey was a student. He seemed to believe, Ramsey remarked some years later, that copies of the Bible in the Authorized Version had rained down from heaven, some with Apocryphas and some without. At the other extreme is the cartoon which depicts God reading a copy of the Bible and muttering darkly, 'I've been misquoted'.

The Bible is set in particular times and specific cultures. It did not drop from heaven as the inspired word of God. That word is given in and through people and events; and as Michael Ramsey has said, 'Truth about God can never be fully expressed in words, not even in inspired words.'[1] As a source of absolute moral laws, the Bible is ambiguous, to say the least; and one of the clearest examples of that ambiguity is its teaching on the position of women in society.

WOMEN IN THE BIBLE

A young woman, with a demanding job, was once asked to read from the book of Proverbs, chapter 31, at a Mothering Sunday family service. She glanced through its eloquent praise of the ideal wife and mother, 'far more precious than jewels', who feeds, clothes and cares for her family with gracious and demure competence. She then scoured her house for different translations of the Bible, trying to find a version which concealed the impact of this idyllic domesticity. As she read them, she slowly realized, to her surprise, that this 'new woman', portrayed in a very old book, also buys property, plants vineyards, makes and sells merchandise. She runs a home and manages various successful business ventures.

The big political question in America, after the election of President Clinton, was whether Hilary Clinton would make cookies or policy. On the campaign trail, she baked cookies, publicly, to burnish the maternal, domestic image. 'She did what she had to,' said one American woman rather crossly. 'She made cookies to get him elected. But now he is elected, I don't want her making hospital visits, I want her to make health care policy.'

The position of women in society, throughout the world, is one of the most pressing questions of justice. In many countries, legislation has been introduced to ensure equality of opportunity and reward for women; but statistics indicate that women are still not as equal as men. In many countries, that very legislation merely reinforces traditional roles. It gives to the mother the right to maternity benefits, and the right to paid leave when children are ill; but because those rights are given to the mother, and are not available to be shared between both the mother and the father, the legislation reinforces the traditional assumption that it is women who do the serious work of parenting, and it is men whose careers and work are to be taken seriously.

In many countries, there is no such legislation at all, and women have little or no power. Mary Grey watched women and young girls walking further and further to find water in the drought-stricken parts of Northern India. They were refused any say in the decision-making processes in their villages because, they were told, water is not women's business.

Professor Grey quotes the Ghanaian theologian, Mercy Aduyoye, writing about motherhood and poverty in the Third World: 'Whatever poverty women as mothers struggle with cannot be understood apart from the real poverty-maker, power, the inability to influence decisions that condition one's life.'[2]

The Jewish and the Christian Scriptures were written in just such a culture. There is no portrait of a 'new man' anywhere in the Bible, parallel to the portrait of the woman in Proverbs 31. But even in that chapter, it is quite clear that the woman's competence serves mainly to enhance the man's standing. She is a precious jewel, in *his* crown. The Bible is written in a patriarchal culture; and there are women, considerable scholars many of them, who argue that if the male-dominated culture of the Bible is put through a sieve, what is left when all the sludge has gone is not glittering gold, but a useless collection of rocks. They wonder how God could ever have made this book the Church's book.[3] But the Bible may be more ambiguous, more positive even about women, than they allow.

IN WHOSE CROWN?

The Book of Genesis contains not one creation story, but two. In the second (2:20-3), the woman is created out of the man, to be his helper ('Why didn't we think of clothes before?' asked Adam, removing Eve's. 'Why did we think of clothes?' said Eve, laundering Adam's).[4] In the first of the creation stories (1: 26-8), both the man and the woman are created together, and are equally blessed.

The law is given on Mount Sinai to the men. It is one of the definitive events of the Old Covenant. The women are not allowed near, and the men are required, for reasons of ritual purity, to keep themselves from women. But the risen Christ appears first to women. It is they who are the first to witness the glory of the New Covenant.

Sarah exists in the Bible as Abraham's wife, her sole function the providing of an heir. When Isaac is born, she fades away. Joseph is Mary's husband. When Jesus is born, Joseph is almost entirely marginalized.

From the birth of Jesus to his death, Mary, not Joseph, is the central figure in his family. The other women who followed Jesus are amongst his most devoted and reliable disciples. Yet Jesus did not choose women to be amongst the twelve. To have done so might have jeopardized his entire mission. In this matter he deferred to the prevailing culture, and chose only men.

In St Paul's teaching, women are free to speak in Church

(1 Corinthians 11:5), but they are also instructed to keep silent (1 Corinthians 14:34). They are subject to men (1 Timothy 2:11-15) and free in Christ (Galatians 3:27-9).

These two strands in the biblical tradition, of which many more examples could be given, were largely interpreted in only one way by the Christian Church. The second Genesis story is used by St Paul and by the Church to keep women in their place. The first is largely forgotten. Mary is exalted as the ideal woman, the virgin mother. Women are thus presented, largely by a male-dominated Church, with an impossible ideal. The tradition of the faithful women who followed Jesus is largely a submerged tradition. Occasionally, though rarely, that submerged stream of women's spirituality and theology surfaces, though generally in a form suitable for consumption in a man's world. The life and work of Teresa of Avila, Julian of Norwich and Hilda of Whitby are conspicuous examples. The Franciscan painter, Fra Angelico, shows the women watching and praying outside the Garden of Gethemane, while the men sleep inside.

BY MEN, AND FOR MEN

Society, marriage, patterns of employment, ownership of property, the life of the Church, theology, practically everything is arranged by men for the benefit of men. God is portrayed, almost invariably, in masculine terms; and inevitably, 'once the Divine is securely identified as male, however subconsciously, women become less divine than men; and for Christianity, that also meant less human. Whether they are despised as 'carnal' or exalted as 'inspiring', they no longer have to be treated as though they were fully human people, made in the image of God.'[5]

For generations, women were denied the right to vote because woman was held to be an inferior form of man. Even in the generation of children, women were held to be passive, since they were thought to provide the physical matter from which the embryo develops, while the man provided the active form and movement. Medieval scholars give the impression that they conceived of the woman's womb as a kind of pressure cooker, from which males emerged well-cooked, firm, and richly-textured. Females were underdone, soft, squidgy, emotional, leaky.[6]

Being weak and vulnerable, prone to tears, women needed strong, male protection, and were treated in law as the property, not the equals, of men. Having little moral sense, they needed men to point them in the right direction. Their creation, out of the side of the man, meant that they shared an image of God through man. Milton summed it all up in the line, 'He for God only, she for God in him'; and he has Eve say to Adam:

> My author and disposer, what thou bidst
> Unargued I obey; so God ordains,
> God is thy law, thou mine: to know no more
> Is woman's happiest knowledge and her praise.'[7]

The Bible is ambiguous, not only because it is the product of a particular culture, but also because it is interpreted by people formed and sustained by a particular tradition. The long and painful struggle to secure equal rights for women in society and in the Church is a struggle made possible only because scientific knowledge about the biology of men and women, and cultural and social change, particularly as a result of the First World War, together with new ways of looking at religious tradition and experience, have all combined in the twentieth century. The submerged traditions of the Bible have only now gained sufficient buoyancy.

The Bible is always read and interpreted in particular circumstances, and by individuals and communities who bring to it all the insights, prejudices and beliefs which they have acquired from the particular society in which they live. At the human level, principles of justice can never be worked out in a vacuum. The Bible itself is the product of human experience.

The Bible is also unique. At the simplest level of historical fact, the Bible is unique because it records and reflects on the long history of a people, in the course of which those people came to know God. There is no other collection of writings which records this story in this way. Whatever view is held about the authority or the inspiration of the Bible, the one basic and indisputable fact is that it stands in a unique relation to those events through which truth about God is revealed. The most important and fundamental question is therefore: what kind of God is revealed to us in the long history of the Jewish and the Christian people? A male God, judge eternal? A God who keeps women in their place? A God who rewards hard work with prosperity and punishes indolence with poverty? A God who commands that we do not resist evil, and that we turn the other cheek? Or a God who fights against evil?

Is God the source of absolute justice? If so, what does justice mean? What answer to that question is offered to us in the Hebrew and the Christian Scriptures?

JUSTICE IN THE HEBREW SCRIPTURES

It was words from the earliest part of that story, the story of Abraham in the book of Genesis, which haunted the Archbishop of York, Dr John Habgood, during the weeks of the Gulf War. He chose them for his text when he preached at the Service of Remembrance and Thanksgiving held in St Mungo's Cathedral, Glasgow, on 4 May, 1991: 'Shall not the judge of all the earth do what is right?' It is Abraham himself, father of Jewish, Christian and Moslem faith, who asks the question which is basic to any understanding of justice in the Hebrew tradition. 'It is a question', said Dr Habgood, 'asked in hope, and in puzzlement.'

The Archbishop supported the need for military action, though he did so with reservations. He was acutely and painfully conscious of the suffering involved – 'the losses of human life and the devastation in Iraq itself, still locked into an oppressive and evil dictatorship; the dreadful plight of the Kurds and Shi'ites; the black clouds over Kuwait, and the oil-sodden Gulf. Behind Abraham's question lies a painful bewildered agonizing. What if doing the right thing not merely fails to stem the tide of suffering but actually extends or diverts it?'

But the question is also asked in hope, 'because the desire to do right, to see justice prevail, to root out wickedness, is not just a human dream, but takes us deep into the heart of God's purposes for his world. It is precisely because there is a judge of all the earth that our striving for a just and peaceful world is not in the end, we believe, a vain delusion.'[8]

Abraham's question is not abstract philosophy. It was of immediate relevance to the fate of those two cities which have become a byword for evil, Sodom and Gomorrah. The story has Abraham pleading with God in a bizarre kind of bargaining, which is intended to establish the actual number of righteous people in the two cities, and the absolute minimum number of people for whose sake the cities will be spared. The number goes down, like a Dutch auction, from fifty to forty-five to forty, and when the number gets down as low as ten, and most of those ten are Lot's family, to whom God has already given 'safe conduct', Abraham ends his questioning and the cities are destroyed. He had only dared to plead with God in the first place because he could not believe that a just God would punish the innocent with the guilty.

The fact that Abraham's question is set in this strange story about two cities is itself significant. Truth is always located in events, and is refined and defined through the telling of story. The story of the feud between Cain and Abel establishes a principle of retribution, powerfully expressed in the Covenant with Noah:

> He who sheds the blood of man
> by man shall his blood be shed
> for in the image of God
> was man created. (Genesis 9:6)

The story of the Exodus is the basis for much of the teaching on social justice, particularly with regard to foreigners: 'Do not oppress an alien; you yourselves know what it feels like to be aliens, because you were aliens in Egypt' (Exodus 23:9). Indeed it is a remarkable fact that commands to love the alien are more frequent in Torah than commands to love your neighbour.

The stories of King David taking the wife of Uriah, and of King Ahab appropriating the vineyard of Naboth, tell that the kings of Israel are neither the source of justice nor above justice, like the sovereigns of other nations, but are themselves subject to the demands of justice.

An understanding of justice does not spring fully formed into the consciousness of the chosen people. The Hebrew people grope their way towards an understanding of justice, through experience, through growing faith, and through many mistakes. Nor do they make that journey of discovery alone. Abraham describes God as judge 'of all the earth'. Babylonian, Egyptian and other cultures of the ancient Near East would have disputed Abraham's belief in one God who is 'Lord of the whole earth'. They thought it likely to be too much for one God, and preferred their more local deities; but they shared an understanding of justice which had much in common with that of the Hebrew people.

The land of Israel was at the meeting point of three great trade routes, and was surrounded by older, more powerful nations. The problems affecting those nations were similar, and there was a general desire for greater social justice. It is therefore hardly surprising that there are close parallels between the Hebrew Scriptures and the codes of law which have come down to us from other ancient civilizations.[9]

THE SOURCE OF JUSTICE

There are, however, two distinctive aspects of Israel's understanding of justice: its source and its purpose. The most fundamental truth is that God is righteous. Not once, not even in the Book of Job, is it suggested that God is unjust. True, God's action, or more especially, God's inaction, caused great bewilderment. The prosperity of the wicked, the suffering of the innocent, the defeat and exile of the whole nation, caused the people of Israel to do some furious questioning. But it was precisely because they clung to the belief that God is righteous that they agonized over apparent unrighteousness.

If they had thought of God as merely the source of righteousness, they might have concluded – as did some of their neighbours – that righteousness is whatever Pharaoh, or the king, acting as or under the inspiration of a deity, happened to command. Righteousness would be entirely arbitrary, as unpredictable as the whims of a divine despot. But Israel came slowly but surely to the belief that God is the source of righteousness, because God is righteous. When Abraham asks, 'Shall not the judge of all the earth do what is right?', he is feeling his way towards that belief.

Somehow he knows, or maybe he just feels intuitively, that to destroy innocent and wicked people together is unjust. But dare he test out that intuition by questioning God? He speaks with great caution, unsure whether the God who has called him is really different from other gods. 'I have taken it upon myself', he says, 'to speak unto the Lord God, I who am but dust and ashes. What if there are just five less than fifty righteous? Will you destroy the whole city because of five people?' His question implies that there is a standard by which even the actions of God may be judged. But to believe in God at all is to believe that there is no source, no life, no being outside of God to which God may be compared.

His questioning is therefore another journey around what is inevitably a circular argument: God is righteous; a righteous God will surely not destroy innocent and wicked together; God does not destroy the innocent with the wicked; therefore God is righteous. Gradually, over the years, out of the stony ground of mixed experience, grew the faith that God is righteous. Not that whatever God happens to command is righteous. But that because God is righteous, the commands of God are just; and the justice of God may eventually be compared, in a specific situation, with the accumulated experience, stretching back over generations, of God as a righteous God.

A COMMUNITY OF RIGHTEOUSNESS

The purpose of righteousness is no less distinctive than this understanding of its source. Its purpose is to link all human beings with one another, and with God, in a relationship of righteous love. Its purpose is far greater than legality, or correct behaviour. To picture God as an impartial judge, measuring behaviour against a set of absolute rules, and dispensing justice in the form of rewards and punishments, is tragically inadequate. Tragically, because it results in false understandings of God and of justice, and opens up a gulf between the Old Testament, harsh, legalistic, and vengeful, and the New Testament, generous, free and full of love.

In both Old and New Testaments, to do justice is to live with God and with other people in relationships of righteous love. Injustice is not primarily the breaking of an absolute ethical standard. It is damage done to the community through a breach in relationships. Every human being lives in a network of differing relationships – in family, school, local community, society, work, each relationship bringing with it specific opportunities. To do justice is to recognize and to meet the opportunities and demands of each different relationship. The standard of behaviour is not some absolute, objective rule which governs relationships. The standard is determined by the relationship itself.

The prophetic movement in Israel calls the people into that true relationship with God which is rooted in holiness, justice and love. The prophet Amos is severe in his passion for justice, condemning the exploitation of the poor, dishonesty in commercial life, and the futility of worship divorced from morality. The prophet Hosea is moving in his portrayal of the strong steadfast love of God, who is passionate, gentle, always faithful. The prophet Isaiah sees both justice and love in his vision of the transcendent majesty of God, whose glory fills the Temple. God's holiness is not the perilous mystery of unpredictable power which must be feared and placated. The transcendent holiness of God is the glory of righteousness and love.

Fundamental to the Hebrew understanding of justice is the recognition that every member of the community of Israel is equal in the sight of God. Equal in creation, equal in slavery in Egypt, equal in deliverance, the people of Israel were united through memory and festival as one chosen race. But theirs was not an egalitarian society in which responsibilities and rewards were shared out equally. Prosperity was honoured, not only as a proper reward for hard work, but also as a sign of God's blessing. Justice in Israel was an attempt to combine the fair distribution of wealth throughout the community on the basis of equality, and a just entitlement to wealth honestly earned.

As in every other society, Jewish law forbids dishonest trading and every kind of exploitation, and offers protection to the most vulnerable and least advantaged people. Similar protection was enshrined in the laws of other nations such as Egypt and Mesopotamia. In one important respect, the laws of some of those other nations were more advanced.

In Babylon and in Assyria, widows and orphans received greater protection than in Israel. But the Hebrew Scriptures go much further than any society known to us in attempting to share wealth fairly throughout the community.

In the earliest stages of their history, the people of Israel were a small, threatened, semi-nomadic people. When they were more settled, they were rooted to the land, a peasant people with a limited agricultural economy. Serious inequalities in wealth or power were no more likely than severe poverty. But gradually, inevitably perhaps, urbanization, commerce, war, and the development of the monarchy, created a new class of wealthy landowners and an underclass of rural poor.

ONE OF THE FINEST BOOKS

The book of Deuteronomy, far from being a boring collection of detailed irrelevancies, is in some ways one of the finest books in the Bible. It retains the ideals of the earlier peasant economy, gathers some of the best insights of the earlier prophetic teaching, combines them with contemporary wisdom, and weaves them into a code of law for the people of the Covenant.

Poverty is considered a scandal, not because it is the failure of individuals, but because it represents an indictment of the whole community. There is no idealizing of poverty – that comes far later in Jewish and Christian thought. The Lord intended blessing for his people, and not poverty. 'There shall be no poor among you', the book of Deuteronomy states confidently, 'if only you will obey the voice of the Lord your God' (15:4–5). But the book is also realistic, and recognizes, just five verses later, that 'the poor will never cease out of the land' (15:11).

The book therefore works at two levels, one concerned with relieving the immediate needs of the poor, the other attempting to change the society which causes or allows poverty. The wealthy are encouraged to 'open wide your hand to the poor' (15:11), a vivid pictorial contrast to the grasping hold of possessions with both hands. The rights of owners and the needs of the poor are both recognized in the practical laws which allow the poor to pick and eat grapes, but not to use any means of carrying quantities away; and to pluck ears of corn, but only by hand, not to harvest them with a sickle.

People who had lost their land often had no alternative but to sell themselves into slavery. The book makes humane provisions for the treatment of such people. These, and many other similar provisions, are rooted in the belief that the whole earth is the Lord's, and the fertile land of Canaan is a particular gift entrusted to all the people of Israel. It is on this same basis that the book includes far-reaching provisions intended to lessen the inequalities which had developed amongst the community. Slaves who escaped were not to be returned into slavery, but were to be helped to find refuge amongst a different group of people. After seven years, all slaves were to be freed, and people released from debt. If money was lent, no interest should be charged. Would you take interest from a brother or sister in your own family? From a foreigner, yes (23: 19-20); but not from a brother Israelite. Every seven years, the harvest was to be grown and then left in the fields, free, for anyone to take.

The most radical provision is not included in Deuteronomy, only in the earlier laws of Leviticus (chapter 25). Perhaps the sheer impossibility of carrying out this ideal had been accepted by the time Deuteronomy was compiled. Every fifty years, there was supposed to be a recognition that all the land belongs to God, and is given leasehold rather than 'in perpetuity'. This belief was expressed in the Year of Jubilee. Every fifty years, all the leases were supposed to run out, and the land revert to the family which first owned it after the Exodus and the entry into Canaan. Whatever would defenders of capitalism, or modern Israel, make of that provision?! Probably they would make most of the fact that it represents a dream which was never realized in practice.

A LIMIT TO INEQUALITY

The purpose of these various provisions was to maintain relationships based on righteousness within the community. If society was not to be divided into extremes of wealth and poverty, some limits on inequality had to be imposed. It was not sufficient simply to provide charitable relief for the poor. Some means of preventing the rich from getting ever richer, while the poor grew poorer, had to be built into the life of society.

To do justice in Israel was to live with God and with other people in relationships of righteous love. But what about the other nations? How far does God's purpose extend? The people of Israel were remarkably privileged. Chosen by God, delivered from Egypt, led to the Promised Land, their extraordinary story prompted the Jews, as it has prompted others, to ask, why? The later history of Israel focused on two contradictory answers, two contrasting ideals. The tension between those two ideals, nationalism and universalism, remains unresolved in Jewish faith. It is a tension already familiar from the attempt to define justice by the use of reason alone. Is privilege the possession of those to whom it is given? Or does justice in relationships require that such privileges are used for the benefit of all?

The nationalist ideal has its roots in Deuteronomy 7, and its continuing expression in some Orthodox Jewish sects living in Israel today. 'You are a people holy to the Lord your God . . . chosen out of all the peoples on the face of the earth to be his people, his treasured possession.' The rest of the chapter is concerned with the separation of Israel from all the other nations, and their eventual destruction.

The universal ideal, also with its counterparts in Israel today, is expressed most powerfully by the prophet Isaiah. Its roots lie in the promise made to Abraham, that 'all peoples on earth will be blessed through you' (Genesis 12:3). Its fulfilment, given poetic expression by Isaiah, lies in establishing relationships of righteousness and peace between all the nations. The banquet of rich food and well-matured wines is hosted by the Lord not only for the chosen people, but for all peoples (Isaiah 25:6-8).

This survey of the Hebrew understanding of righteousness began with Abraham's question, 'Shall not the judge of all the earth do what is right?' It is a question, said the Archbishop of York, asked in hope and in puzzlement. So far, this account of justice in Judaism has concentrated largely on hope. Abraham was soon to be caught up in bewildering injustice, and overwhelmed by puzzlement.

The Biblical narrative contains two accounts of gross injustice. Both are presented as being the will of God. Both are central to Biblical faith. One is the sacrifice of Isaac, the other the sacrifice of Christ. Some detailed consideration of both accounts may reveal something of that likeness of the God of justice which has always been there, painted on the

Biblical canvas, but which is too easily obscured beneath layers of unthinking piety.

'TAKE YOUR SON ISAAC AND SACRIFICE HIM AS A BURNT OFFERING'

The walls of the Etchmiadzin Chapel in the Armenian Orthodox Church in the Old City of Jerusalem are decorated with a large collection of curious tiles. Each one is hand-painted, some with great artistry, others crudely done. The washing of the feet of the disciples shows Peter, one foot hovering above the basin, one finger scratching the top of his head, face a study in utter bewilderment. John the Baptist is crudely beheaded with a curved scimitar by Turkish soldiers wearing pantaloons, an interpretation which owes more to the enmity between the Armenians and the Turks than to historical fact.

The sacrifice of Isaac is depicted with such crude simplicity that it makes comic a chilling story. Abraham is a benign, venerable figure, untroubled by the enormity of what God requires of him. Isaac kneels bound on the stones, blindfolded, his features scarcely defined at all. The knife floats in the air. A ram, curiously shaped, hangs by its horns from the lower branches of a palm tree, like washing on a line, so far off the ground that only a most remarkable jump could have carried it there. There is no urgency in the drawing, no horror. It prompts no questions, only a wry smile.

Chaim Potock has a far darker version in his novel, *The Gift of Asher Lev*. An Orthodox Jew from Brooklyn, Asher Lev is an artist who has achieved fame internationally but only uncomprehending notoriety in his own Jewish community, mainly for his two paintings, The Brooklyn Crucifixions. Later he works on another huge canvas depicting the sacrifice of Isaac. His wife watches in tense silence as he brings the painting to life, only her eyes telling how much she dislikes it. Then his father calls, and stares in trembling anger and bewilderment at the finished canvas. 'What have you done?' he cries. 'He did not kill him. This is what you will show the world? Abraham slaughtering Isaac?' Asher Lev replies, 'It's how I feel about it.'[10]

Perhaps for a majority of people the sacrifice of Isaac is made tolerable by the fact that it did not actually happen. The ram was already caught in a thicket, proof that God had made advance plans to stay Abraham's hand at the last moment. For Asher Lev, such a last-minute reprieve is intolerable if it is used to vindicate a cruel act of injustice. Better if Isaac had been sacrificed. Otherwise the whole story is strangely reminiscent of those times when the hostages in Lebanon, Waite, Keenan, and the others, were taken out blindfolded, had a gun pressed to their heads, were told they would die, and then heard the explosion of a blank cartridge or the click of a firing pin.

A curious, more light-hearted version of the sacrifice being called off is shown in a tapestry in the Jesuit House in Trier. Isaac is bound on the altar as usual, but Abraham has no knife. Instead, he takes careful aim with a seventeenth-century flintlock pistol. An angel takes equally careful aim. Like a schoolboy, the angel pees in a high trajectory which splashes down on the firing pin of the pistol. A couplet reads:

> Abraham you aim in vain,
> An angel sends a little rain.

TESTED TO THE POINT OF DESTRUCTION

The ram provided as an alternative for sacrifice may have been a divine contingency plan; but the whole point of the story is that Abraham did not know, as we do, how the story would end. Nor did God know in advance what Abraham would do. Abraham is tested with great severity, almost to the point of destruction, because so much is at stake, and because God does not know how he will respond. The narrative in Genesis 22 makes clear how important is this testing of Abraham, but gives no ground at all for thinking that God knew what the outcome would be.

The promise made by God to Abraham was a solemn covenant. His descendants would be like the sand on the seashore. The child, Isaac, given to Abraham and Sarah in their old age, is the child of promise. Through this child, God says, my promise to you will be fulfilled. Then God commands Abraham to kill Isaac. It is nonsensical. Or, in the more measured words of Martin Luther, there is here 'a contradiction, with which God contradicts himself'.

God's command to Abraham may be a horrifying nonsense, but Abraham responds not with anger or incredulity, but with active submission. 'Early the next morning' he starts chopping wood, so that after he has killed Isaac he will be able to burn his body as a sacrifice to God. The narrative does not tell us whether Abraham had slept well the previous night. Nor whether he raised any objections to this new twist in the divine plan. Nor are we told whether he had any discussion with his wife Sarah, who might also have had some view about the impending death, at his father's hand, of this treasured son of her old age. She does not feature in the account at all.

Even Isaac is allowed only one question. He has noticed

the wood (perhaps he helped to gather it) but wonders where the sacrifice is. Abraham stalls. Yet by the standards of many victims, Isaac does well. He is at least able to ask something. Victims are often silent, or silenced. Though they know more than anyone about injustice, the voices of the victims are seldom heard.

C. S. Lewis, groping his way through the dark agonies of bereavement, once remarked: 'Not that I am (I think) in much danger of ceasing to believe in God. The real danger is of coming to believe such dreadful things about him. The conclusion I dread is not "so there's no God after all", but "so this is what God's really like. Deceive yourself no longer." '[11] Did Abraham have similar dark thoughts as he walked with Isaac, carrying a knife and a bundle of firewood?

Abraham, after a long walk, reaches the place of sacrifice, binds his son, presumably also blindfolds him (did Isaac think this was a game?) and raises his knife. At that moment, with only seconds to spare, Abraham is stopped. An angel shouts his name twice. He has passed the test. 'Now I know', says the angel, 'that you fear God.' He did indeed.

Some time later God has a few quiet words with Isaac, the unwitting victim of this set piece. 'I will make your descendants as numerous as the stars in the sky', God promises 'and will give them all these lands and through your offspring all nations on earth will be blessed, because Abraham obeyed me.'[12] Diplomatically, perhaps, God does not mention that because of that very obedience, Isaac had been within seconds of death.

It is almost impossible for us to grasp the sheer horror of this episode. We know, and have always known, how the story ends. Is it not one of the great examples of faith? But the test itself, whatever the outcome, was by any normal standards a grievous act of injustice. Does the end ever justify the means?

The story is sometimes explained as an example of the ending of child sacrifice. Abraham follows the pagan customs prevalent in his time, and decides to offer his son as a sacrifice. God stops him. Child sacrifice is not to be part of the life of the chosen people, and by putting his faith in God even when his sacrifice is refused, Abraham passes the test. There is just one problem with this explanation, namely that it is not what the text says. The story begins not with Abraham's decision to offer his son, but with God commanding Abraham to do so. If God is the source of absolute justice, how are we to understand this act of injustice?

If justice requires that a person must always receive what he or she deserves, then Abraham received rather more than he deserved. If justice demands a strict adherence to what is right and a rejection of what is wrong, then the God who commands Abraham to commit so great an act of injustice cannot be the source of absolute justice. Evidently God has other considerations in mind which are more important than justice, which can override the demands of strict justice, and which are higher than the ideals of justice.

The best clue to understanding all this is provided in the letter of James. It is not strict justice which is at stake here, but righteousness. Abraham has been called into an extraordinary relationship with God, one which therefore makes unusual demands. Rabbi Jonathan Magonet points out that God does not command Abraham to offer his son as a sacrifice, as most translations imply. God asks him. The opening words of the story, 'Please take your son . . .', suggest that there is much at stake for God here too.[13] When

Abraham does exactly what is required, he meets the demands of the relationship. He trusts God; 'and the Scripture was fulfilled that says, Abraham believed God, and it was credited to him as righteousness' (James 2:21-3).

James adds a phrase which indicates how close was the relationship between Abraham and God: 'He was called God's friend'. No-one else in the Old Testament is described by God as 'Abraham, my friend' (Isaiah 41:8). The demands of righteous love generated by so close a relationship were bound to be quite extraordinary.

A great American theologian, Reinhold Niebuhr, once made a somewhat puzzling remark which has often been quoted: 'Any justice which is only justice soon degenerates into something less than justice. It must be saved by something which is more than justice.'[14]

Niebuhr's statement is included in a discussion of social and individual morality. 'From the perspective of society,' he writes, 'the highest moral ideal is justice. From the perspective of the individual, the highest ideal is unselfishness. The individual must strive to realize his life by losing and finding himself in something greater.'[15] Abraham was asked, by God, to run the risk of losing the promise for which he had lived. In taking the risk of losing his life, he found himself 'in something greater'. Was justice redeemed, in the end, by that righteousness which includes, and is greater than, justice?

JUSTICE IN CHRISTIAN FAITH

The story of Abraham is used not only by James, but also by St Paul, to link together the Hebrew and the Christian understandings of righteousness. The decisive quotation,

'Abraham believed the Lord; and he credited it to him as righteousness', occurs first not in the letter of James, but in the middle of the story of Abraham (Genesis 15:6). St Paul uses the same quotation in his letter to the Galatians, and again in writing to the Christians in Rome. It focuses the heart of the Christian Gospel.

The question St Paul addresses is the most profound and the most simple question of all. On what basis is a relationship with God to be established? That is the central question of the Christian Scriptures. The answer to that question provides the context, the framework within which the Christian teaching on justice must be understood.

St Paul traces the unfolding of that answer through the history which runs from Abraham to Christ, and which it is possible to summarize, albeit inadequately, in two paragraphs.

God, in love freely given, chose Abraham and established through him a covenant relationship with the people of Israel. God promised to be their God, to love them, protect them and lead them. Israel promised to be God's people, and to worship and serve God alone. Gradually, over the years, the behaviour and way of life of individuals and of the whole people was set out in the law. Through weakness, disobedience and wickedness, Israel repeatedly broke this covenant. God, in love, repeatedly forgave and restored.

But that repeated failure resulted in a distortion of the purpose for which the law had been given. Instead of being received joyfully as a gift, the law was felt to be an imposition. Instead of being an expression of life in a covenant relationship, it was perverted into a means whereby that relationship might be earned. But once the covenant relationship is broken, it can be restored only by God's forgiveness. In the life and death of Christ, God makes a new covenant, freely available to everyone. Like the old covenant first made with Abraham, who trusted in God, it is a relationship based not on obedience to law, but on faith. To trust in God is to enter into a relationship with the God who is both justice and love.

It is only within this framework that the apparent contradictions within the teaching of St Paul, and of Jesus too, can be understood. Early in his letter to the Romans, Paul asks whether the law is overthrown by this faith. 'Not at all!' he replies. 'On the contrary, we uphold the law' (Romans 3:31). Seven chapters later, he declares that 'Christ is the end of the law, that everyone who believes may be made righteous' (10:4).

Jesus says that he has come not to destroy the law and the prophets, but to fulfil them (Matthew 5:17). Yet his words and actions appear to overthrow the law. There is a crisp saying which neatly harmonizes these contrasts: The law was given that grace might be sought; grace was given that the law might be fulfilled. Though true, that saying is too neat. It fails to struggle with the contradictions, and so misses the depths in Jesus' teaching.

On the one hand, Jesus respects and values the teaching, the culture and the way of life represented by the law and the prophets. He does not ignore and go racing past it, knocking everything over in a revolutionary rush towards a new future. On the other hand, he reaches so deeply into the tradition that his teaching is radically new, so new that it cannot be combined with the old.

He is so concerned for justice that he refuses to lead any revolutionary movement which might only result in greater injustices. Yet his life and teaching reach beyond justice into that righteous love which is radically disturbing.

Jesus offers no political manifesto, no programme for

reform, no blueprint for a new social order. He is not a revolutionary hero, offering himself as a martyr in the cause of a new, just future. Yet his teaching is so subversive of religious and political authority that he ends up a political prisoner, in direct and open conflict with all the people who hold power.

A MILITARY MOVEMENT

One event, so challenging and significant that it is recorded in all four gospels, is presented to us as an occasion when Jesus could have become the leader of a revolutionary movement. The feeding of the five thousand was not the gentle but unusual outdoor picnic so often described. It was far more than a remarkable thanksgiving barbecue. It was a decisive event which required great skills in leadership.

St Mark tells us that there were five thousand men present. Women and children were there too, but they would not be expected to follow Jesus in a popular revolt against the Roman power. The people all listened to Jesus with mounting excitement. Then, to establish some control, Jesus makes everyone sit down. They may have sat in groups, but the word is ambiguous and suggests that the great gathering may have sat in ranks, forming a ragged hollow square more suitable to a military assembly than a large cluster of family picnics.

They had been with Jesus and away from home for three days. Anything they might have brought with them had already been eaten. Yet the five loaves and the two fish provided food for everyone; and as the fragments were being collected, the excitement and the whispering grew until it became a great force. The people who had shared this

Messianic banquet began to surge forward to acknowledge and claim their leader. St John tells us that 'they wanted to take him by force to make him their king' (John 6:15). Jesus immediately takes evasive action. He orders his disciples (the word is unusually strong – he had to compel them) to get into a boat and go. His lieutenants then have to watch from the sea, powerless, as Jesus, with magisterial authority, dismisses the crowd and then goes away by himself into the hills.

The story is a clear rejection by Jesus of the role of the revolutionary leader who will bring in a new, just order by defeating the injustice of the Roman occupation. It is perhaps hardly surprising that his rejection of this role resulted in a sharp decline in his popularity. 'After this, many of his disciples drew back and no longer went with him,' St John tells us; and a few verses later Jesus makes particular mention of Judas, aware that his disappointment may have been most acute (John 6:66-71).

Yet it is clear, from his life and teaching, and from the rest of the New Testament, that Jesus is profoundly concerned about justice, though not as a cause, or a movement, or a programme, or a revolution. He is primarily concerned about justice between people in relationships. His radical teaching embraces but moves beyond strict justice into that righteous love which is the source of justice.

The Sermon on the Mount is full of sayings which may be summarized in the words 'Not simply . . . but more'. Not simply justice, but more than justice: not merely 'do not kill', but don't even think about it, or about revenge, or even anger . . . be reconciled to your brother; not simply, 'do not commit adultery', but do not even fantasize about that other woman; not simply legitimate and just revenge – an eye for an eye – but love your enemies; not simply carrying the baggage for the one mile which a Roman soldier could demand, but two miles; not simply your coat, if someone would take it, but your cloak too.

As under the old covenant, so in the new, justice is part of that righteous love which is the heart and being of God. To be perfect, as your Father in heaven is perfect (Matthew 5:48) is not an ideal to be achieved step by step. It is a state of being, an expression of that wholeness which flows from a relationship with God. Jesus allows no distinction between motive and action. What you are is what you do, and what you think and desire is what you are. Love God. Love your neighbour. That is all. In these two commandments, all the law and the prophets are included.

In these two commandments also, that tension which persists in the Hebrew Scriptures, between nationalism and universalism, is resolved. Jesus does not ignore the boundaries between Jew and Arab, Samaritan and Jew, brother and enemy; but his command is that love should penetrate those boundaries, and offer our neighbour that same love with which we love ourselves.

The purpose of God's righteous love, in both Jewish and Christian faith, is beautifully summed up in the story of Jonah. Commanded by God to take a message of fire and brimstone to Nineveh, a city of pagan foreigners, the Jewish prophet is understandably put out. When eventually, via storm and fish, he reaches the city, and delivers his message with all the enthusiasm he can manage, the people repent. God forgives them. There is no brimstone. Jonah is furious.

'I always knew you were like that,' Jonah fumes, 'a God who is gracious and compassionate, slow to anger and abounding in steadfast love.' Whether Jonah himself ever got the message, as he sat in the shade of the plant God thoughtfully provided, is never made clear. A world which lives in the shadow of the Cross should be able to recognize the love of God more readily. But like the plant, which grew and then withered, leaving Jonah baffled in the hot sun, the Cross of Christ is an ambiguous, puzzling sign of God's justice.

ANOTHER FINAL NIGHT

The parallels between the sacrifice of Isaac and the sacrifice of Christ are close, so close as to be almost uncanny. Yet again the will of God involves an act of horrendous injustice. Christ, like Abraham, was tested to the point of destruction. He too passed the test; and once more, the horror of what happened is obscured by our knowledge of the outcome.

We may know little about what Abraham thought in the night before he set out with Isaac; but we do know something of what Jesus thought and said in the night in which he was betrayed. He took bread, broke it, and gave it to his bewildered disciples with the stark words: 'This is my body, broken for you.' He took a cup of wine, and perhaps poured a little, very slowly, on to the table. Then he told his disciples to drink it. 'This', he said, 'is my blood, poured out for many for the forgiveness of sins.'

For months, Jesus has lived with the chilling knowledge that his work will almost certainly end in a violent death. The gospels indicate a growing conviction that this death will be neither an accident, nor a tragic mistake, nor a desperate attempt to further his cause by martyrdom. His death will be the will of God. The Psalms which Jesus knew so well that he quoted them from memory, and the prophecies of Isaiah, pointed to the death of the servant of the Lord, a death which would be violent, horrible, and the will of God.

From the upper room in which the Last Supper was held, Jesus walked through the dark, narrow streets of Jerusalem, streets which are never wholly silent. He was with friends, and utterly alone. So far as he was aware, not one person, out of the thousands who had heard him, had grasped the real meaning of the Kingdom. Not even one of the disciples had understood. Perhaps Judas had come closest to recognizing the truth about the Messiah, but for him it was too much of a reversal of everything he had expected. So Judas was out there, somewhere in the darkness, betraying the man by whom he himself felt betrayed. The other eleven still walked with Jesus, probably a little way behind him. They had eaten well, drunk well, it was late, they were tired, and they were caught up in events they feared and did not understand. To be in the midst of friends who do not begin to understand is to experience deep and terrible loneliness.

The small group passed quietly through one of the city gates, and out into the Kidron Valley. What happens next is not a well-ordered prayer meeting in a borrowed garden, but a black night of desperate fear. Jesus passes through the dark, silent graveyards below the Mount of Olives, a bad experience at the best of times, terrible for one who knows that his hour has come. He stumbles into the Garden of Gethsemane, chilled by the sweat of fear, desperate in his loneliness. He pleads with his closest friends to stay with him, knowing that it is futile to expect anything more of them. Then he staggers away and falls to the ground. Is it too much to suggest that Jesus experiences something of a breakdown? Is this what is meant by those verses, added later to St Luke's account, which tell that his sweat 'was like great drops of blood falling to the ground' (Luke 22:43-4)?

Are the 'loud cryings and tears' mentioned in the letter to the Hebrews the agonies of a man struggling desperately with dread? The measured words which have come down to us – 'Father, if you are willing, take this cup from me; yet not my will but yours be done' – inevitably disguise the horror. The will of God is brutal, cruel, and utterly unjust. How can it be the will of God? Has God forgotten justice? Or can justice be saved by something which is more than justice?

Again, as with the story of Abraham, our understanding of the last hours of Jesus' life is not filled with darkness and fearful uncertainty, but with the light and understanding which break through from the Resurrection. How can such a glorious end do other than justify the dreadful means by which it is achieved?

It is too easy, knowing the end, to pass over the injustice through which that end was achieved. But by any standards, the death of Jesus is a perversion of justice. Here is a man, a good man by all accounts, who is a threat to the religious authorities. He is arrested, and tried in a way which is open to serious objection by the standards of Jewish law. He is declared, by the Roman authority, to be not guilty. He is then crucified in response to mob rule. If this is the will of God, then as with the sacrifice of Isaac, there must be other considerations in the mind and will of God which override the demands of strict justice.

A DEMONSTRATION OF JUSTICE

The Christian tradition does include one significant strand of thinking which interprets the death of Jesus as the supreme act of divine justice. The death of Jesus is a sacrifice, perfect in every respect, offered to God in total obedience. This is one of the great themes of the New

Testament, particularly of the letter to the Hebrews. St Paul summarizes concisely in his letter to the Romans when he writes: 'God presented Jesus as a sacrifice of atonement through faith in his blood. He did this to demonstrate his justice, because in his forbearance he had left the sins committed beforehand unpunished. He did this to demonstrate his justice at the present time, so as to be just and the one who justifies those who have faith in Jesus' (Romans 3:25-6). The sacrifice of an unblemished animal as a way of dealing with sin is here transferred to the death of Jesus.

Justice requires that sin is treated with the utmost seriousness; and the death of Jesus demonstrates, for all time, the justice of God. Justice allows neither cheap grace nor easy forgiveness. It involves the very life of God. In offering himself as a 'full, perfect and sufficient sacrifice, oblation and satisfaction for the sins of the whole world',[16] Jesus has both suffered and demonstrated the ultimate cost of forgiveness. The demands of justice, that evil be taken seriously, are met.

But interpreting the death of Jesus as a sacrifice for sin has also brought with it ideas of punishment. St Paul's use of the word in the passage quoted is sometimes understood to mean that Jesus died as the ultimate punishment for all human sin. If God was in Christ, then God, in this man Jesus, has borne the punishment due to us. In this way, God is said to have satisfied the demands of justice by paying the ultimate penalty. It is as if the judge were to pronounce the death sentence on a man found guilty of murder, and then himself take the place of the guilty man. The judge goes to the gallows, and the guilty man goes free.

The problems associated with this understanding are immense. It raises the obvious questions about whether the death of one man, however good, however innocent, is sufficient punishment for the evil done by all people in all times, a question which is unanswerable. That it may be asked is an inevitable consequence of understanding the death of Jesus as some kind of transaction.

THE JUST FOR THE UNJUST

More serious still, how can the demands of justice be met by an innocent man suffering instead of the guilty? The ten people who are known as the Guildford Four and the Birmingham Six have hard personal experience of this question. All ten were arrested, tried, imprisoned, subsequently found not guilty, and released. Some reflection on their experience may shed light on the question of whether justice can ever be served by the innocent suffering in the place of the guilty.

The bombing of the two Birmingham pubs in 1974 was deeply shocking to the whole world, but particularly so to those of us who lived in Birmingham at the time, and who worked in the city centre. The wave of grief and anger which engulfed the city was overwhelming in its power and in its demand that the evil people that had done this terrible thing be brought to justice. By the time the staffs of the pubs gathered in St Martin's-in-the-Bull Ring for a service of prayer, shortly after the bombings, six men had been arrested. The imprisonment of the Birmingham Six, the recognition years later that they were innocent, and their subsequent release from prison, is now a notorious episode in British justice. No-one could possibly suggest that the imprisonment and the punishment of those six innocent men has in any way atoned for the evil of the bombings. The demands of justice cannot be met by the innocent suffering instead of the guilty.

But suppose the Six had not been wrongly arrested, but had offered themselves as scapegoats, as a willing sacrifice to atone for the evil? The very idea is a nonsense in the strict sense of that word. The response from all of us in Birmingham, as in the nation, would have been the same then as it is in fact now after the release of the Six; a demand that the guilty be found and punished. The idea that the innocent may bear the punishment due to the guilty is not an expression of justice. It is deeply subversive of justice. If the death of Christ is interpreted as God punishing the innocent instead of the guilty, then justice itself is undermined. This interpretation is not an indication of that righteous love which reaches beyond justice, or of justice being saved by a love which is more than justice. It is so much less than justice that both justice and righteous love are subverted.

What then is the connection between the justice of God and the death of Jesus? The Birmingham Six and their families have been deeply wronged. They can respond to that wrong at different levels. They can, and should, seek for justice. They deserve full compensation. Justice requires that the actions of those who brought them to trial should be carefully examined. The fact that British courts have decided that the case cannot proceed against the police who were responsible, because now they could not have a fair trial, is both an expression of justice and a frustration of justice. It is important also to observe that the attitudes of those of us who lived in Birmingham at the time require careful and critical examination; for the palpable anger in the city required the police not simply to do something, but anything.

The Six can and should seek justice. But 'justice which is only justice soon degenerates into something less than justice. It must be saved by something which is more than justice.'[17] It is not simply a matter of justice. It is also a matter of righteousness, of what is required if such complex and tortured relationships are ever to be opened up to healing demands of righteous love.

At that deeper level of righteousness, the Six have to make the hard choice of whether or not to forgive what was done to them. If they can, they will be free, for to forgive is to let go of the hurt and the bitterness. But to forgive also means that they must bear the cost of that forgiveness themselves, the cost of those lost years, the separation from their families, and the wrongful imprisonment, for which no financial compensation can possibly be adequate. If they can forgive the society which so wronged them, then the people in that society too may move to a level deeper than justice, and may be able to forgive themselves for the way in which those men and their families have been treated.

STRANGELY APPROPRIATE

The death of Jesus is an act of injustice which makes forgiveness necessary and shows that forgiveness is possible. The fact that it was the will of God, and that God's will was achieved through betrayal by Judas, injustice in the Jewish courts, and weakness on the part of Pilate, is strangely appropriate. For injustice of this kind is part of that evil which God wills to confront. But at a level deeper than strict justice, the death of Christ is an act of forgiveness rooted in righteous love. It is God, in Christ, showing what is always true; that forgiveness is terribly costly, and that God always bears the cost of that forgiveness.

The death of Christ is not a once for all transaction by which justice is done and the punishment for sin is laid upon the innocent instead of the guilty. The Cross shows, in human life, what is always true, that injustice and sin and evil are a rejection of the love of God; and that God, in love, bears the cost of that rejection in order that forgiveness might always be possible, and relationships of righteous love may be restored.

'On this cross', writes John Baker, 'God fulfils the nature of forgiveness by using the evil done to him as the means to a new good; for it is the cross of Jesus which creates within me a free, unhesitating acceptance of the law of love.'[18]

If justice were all, who could stand? That is a constant theme in the Psalms and in the Hebrew Scriptures. Justice requires that every person should receive what he or she deserves. Hence the anxious prayer of the Psalmist: 'If thou Lord should be extreme to mark what is done amiss, O Lord who may abide it. But there is mercy with Thee. Therefore shalt thou be feared.'

Even the divine justice might degenerate into something less than justice if it were only justice. The death of Jesus is an act of justice that is more than justice. The Scriptures nowhere tell that 'God is justice'. They do say that 'God is love'. That great truth does not subvert justice; but justice is saved by the love which is more than justice.

At the heart of the Hebrew and the Christian Scriptures is not legalism, nor an awesome Judge, but a joyful recognition that the ultimate reality is righteous love. Justice is an appearance of love in human society. It is righteous love in action. It is by the standards of the righteous love of God that every attempt at justice in human society is to be judged.

These two great acts of righteous love, the binding of Isaac and the sacrifice of Christ, must mean that absolute justice cannot be the final word. Through them we perceive something greater than justice. We will explore the implications of this in the next chapter. For if absolute justice is not the ultimate reality, then it must surely follow that absolute right and absolute wrong cannot be the last word either. Right and wrong are appropriate to matters of justice, and love is to be expressed not only in the more simple terms of right and wrong, but also in ways which are good. The death of Christ, like the sacrifice of Isaac, is both wrong and good; an act of injustice through which justice is ultimately revealed as righteous love.

THREE

LOVE TO DO JUSTICE

Mrs Lilian Boyes died in August 1991 at the hands of her doctor. Her death was not an unfortunate medical accident. It was deliberate. Dr Nigel Cox, the doctor who brought her life to an end, was brought to trial, and was found guilty of attempted murder. On 22 September 1992, he was sentenced to twelve months' imprisonment, suspended for twelve months.

The case brought urgent moral questions into sharp focus, among them the question of the relation between love and justice. Many people found themselves thinking, somewhat uncomfortably, that the death of Mrs Boyes was both wrong and good. For them, the deliberate ending of her life was an act of compassion which was legally wrong and morally good. Others thought it was simply wrong, both legally and morally. The deep and strong feelings aroused by that case surface again whenever euthanasia is discussed. The facts of the case, which aroused international concern, are probably not remembered so clearly.

Mrs Boyes had been a patient of Dr Cox for thirteen years. She was seventy years old, and for many years she had suffered from what a professor of rheumatology described as 'the most severe case of rheumatoid arthritis I have ever read about'. The physical symptoms, particularly in the final months of her life, were appalling, too dreadful even to record in detail. It is enough to say that even the gentlest touch caused her such pain that she screamed: 'like a dog', said one of her nurses.

Dr Cox had promised Mrs Boyes that she would die peacefully; but she was not dying peacefully. She was dying a terrible and miserable slow death. Eventually, in some despair, Dr Cox gave her a lethal injection of potassium chloride. The injection had no curative or painkilling properties. The intention was to end her life. But no one could be certain whether her death, minutes after the injection, was due to the injection itself or to the illness. The charge therefore had to be one of attempted murder.

The prosecution had to establish that Dr Cox had intended to kill Mrs Boyes. The defence could not deny the intention, and argued instead that the motives and the results of the injection were good, a few minutes of freedom from pain during which Mrs Boyes grasped her son's hand, then the release of death. Three members of the jury were in tears when the guilty verdict was returned.

There is little doubt, from all the available evidence, that Dr Cox acted in what he believed to be the best interest of his patient. Nevertheless, the law required, as a matter of justice, that he be found guilty. The fact that he acted out of a genuine concern for his patient was reflected in the suspended prison sentence. But was he also guilty in the sight of God? Did he act against divine, as well as human, justice?

Contrary to what is often supposed, neither the Jewish nor the Christian tradition gives absolute value to human life. Here too, it appears, absolute justice does not exist. There is no absolute obligation to preserve human life at all costs. If there were, it would lead to untold suffering for sick and elderly people. In addition to this consideration, there are circumstances in which the deliberate ending of life is the lesser of two evils. War is the most obvious example.

THE VALUE OF LIFE

The Christian tradition does not place an absolute value on human life. Instead, it gives a very high value to human life. It recognizes that all human life is a gift of God, and that every human being is to be valued equally, without regard to age or infirmity, gender or race, social status or usefulness. Christian faith also insists that people who are particularly vulnerable through illness or disability are to be given special care and protection. Anyone who deliberately ends the life of another human being, or who fails to protect the life of another person, must be required to give account to appropriate legal authorities. That is precisely what happened in the case of Dr Cox.

Justice demands that the right to life of every human being should be respected, and that life may not be deliberately ended except in strictly defined circumstances. But it is out of that very same respect for life that pressure arises to extend the defined circumstances. Mrs Boyes wanted the doctor to end her life. So did her family. Euthanasia has been defined as the deliberate ending of life because that is the only way, in the circumstances, to enable the person to die with dignity and in peace.

Lilian Boyes was so ravaged by illness that she had neither dignity nor peace. She pleaded with doctors to end her life. But the Christian tradition does not allow that individuals have any absolute right to decide when to die. Nor does it give to people, pregnant women, for example, an absolute right to decide what should happen to their own bodies. This is mainly because of the respect due to human life, whether one's own or someone else's, as a gift from God. It is also because no individual can act in isolation, and one individual deciding when to die affects the whole of society. Also, an absolute right to decide when to die would, to be effective, require the assistance of other people in some circumstances; and no human being can require such assistance of another in the act of death. It is for these reasons that the personal views of an individual have not been given absolute value in the Christian tradition.

Modern culture now puts sharp questions to that tradition. Many women in particular demand the right to decide whether or not to remain pregnant. Banners carried in pro-abortion marches proclaim, 'Not the Church, Not the State, Let the woman decide her fate.'

The technology available in modern medicine also challenges the tradition. Patients are now kept alive, artificially, when previously they would have died. It is well known that doctors are deliberately ending the lives of terminally ill patients by giving larger doses of painkilling drugs than are strictly necessary for the relief of pain. Indeed, one of the criticisms of Dr Cox, made privately by some doctors, was that he did not end the life of Mrs Boyes earlier by the administration of such drugs. Even with the best possible terminal care, in a hospice, where there is skill and experience in the relief of pain, and where every individual is valued and respected, there are circumstances where patients are so ill that they have neither dignity nor peace. Respect for them, as human beings, would seem to require not merely the passive removal of medical treatment, but the deliberate, active ending of life.

MORE, NOT LESS, THAN JUSTICE

This brief review of a tragic case, and of the wider considerations, bears directly on the relation between love and justice. It is not adequate, nor even safe, to suggest that if love is the motive, the action will be good. Even if, as with Dr Cox, the motive is one of love, the action may still be considered wrong. Love must be expressed, in society, through justice. That demands a profound respect for the value and dignity of human life. But there are differing views about how that value and dignity are to be respected at the end of life.

There is the traditional view that the deliberate ending of life is wrong; and there is the view that in certain circumstances the deliberate ending of life is necessary to enable a person to die with dignity and in peace. For some, there is no question. Justice demands such respect for the value of human life in the individual and in society that the deliberate ending of life is always wrong. Love requires that everything possible should be done to ease suffering and to care for the dying, short of ending life deliberately. On this view, justice and love are one.

For others, justice and love also mean that every human being must be valued and respected, and that everything possible must be done to ease suffering and to give care to those who are dying; but when everything possible has been done, there may still be dreadful suffering, in which case the deliberate ending of life is both necessary and good. Strict justice may require that life is preserved, but if there is such suffering that respect for human life demands a dignified and peaceful end to that suffering, then justice must be saved by love, though by a love which is more, not less, than justice.

In Holland, as in Britain, euthanasia is illegal. Yet doctors in Holland deliberately end the lives of around 4,000 people each year, and it is extremely rare for any of those doctors to be prosecuted. Towards the end of 1993, the Dutch Government, by a narrow majority, gave legal approval to some clear guidelines. A twenty-eight point checklist has been published, and the Government has given assurances to doctors that if they follow the guidelines carefully, they will not be prosecuted. In this way, the traditional demands of strict justice are upheld. Every time a doctor ends life, he must report in detail to the Public Prosecutor who has to decide in each case whether to initiate legal action.

Yet the deliberate ending of life is not only possible in Holland. It is widely practised. Doctors value the possibility, because it is, in some circumstances, the final act of loving service they can render to their patients. Patients value it because, within carefully defined circumstances, they are free to choose to end their lives with dignity and in peace. But doctors find the legal position seriously unsatisfactory. Their work falls somewhere between tolerance and crime. They are in an exposed area between two frontiers, between an understanding of justice which cannot yet let them go, and an understanding of love which beckons them towards a new frontier.

That new frontier may prove to be at the top of an extremely slippery slope. What was thought to be love may then prove to be a treacherous sentiment. There are many people in Holland, doctors among them, who are uneasy. Some are strongly opposed to the new policy. They point out that in Nazi Germany, costly medical treatment was withdrawn first from the incurable, then from the handicapped, then from the elderly and infirm. Once let go of strict justice, and anything might happen.

Elizabeth Jennings wrote a poem in which she imagines what the legalizing of euthanasia would do to elderly people, living in a nursing home:

> The law's been passed and I am lying low
> Hoping to hide from those who think they are
> Kindly, compassionate. My step is slow.
> I hurry. Will the executioner
> Be watching how I go?

Others about me clearly feel the same.
The deafest one pretends that she can hear.
The blindest hides her white stick while the lame
Attempt to stride. Life has become so dear.
Last time the doctor came

All who could speak said they felt very well.
Did we imagine he was watching with
A new deep scrutiny? We could not tell.
Each minute now we think the stranger Death
Will take us from each cell

For that is what our little rooms now seem
To be. We are prepared to bear much pain,
Terror attacks us wakeful, every dream
Is now a nightmare. Doctor's due again.
We hold on to the gleam

Of sight, a word to hear. We act, we act,
And doing so we wear our weak selves out.
We said 'We want to die' once when we lacked
The chance of it. We wait in fear and doubt.
O life, you are so packed

With possibility. Old age seems good.
The ache, the anguish – we could bear them, we
Declare. The ones who pray plead with their God
To turn the murdering ministers away,
But they come softly-shod.[1]

On this view, the murdering ministers, still 'softly-shod', would soon extend their ministry from the terminally ill who want to die, to those with Alzheimer's who are a long time dying, to the severely handicapped who cannot tell what they want, to those whose old age is inconvenient for others. It is not safe to let go of traditional understandings of strict justice without having a firm hold on righteous love; or the end result may be neither justice nor love.

THE SUPREME VIRTUE

Clearly the relation between love and justice is of great significance. For Greek thinkers such as Plato and Aristotle, it is justice, and not love, which is the supreme virtue in society. They cannot agree on the other virtues, but they are at least agreed on the supremacy of justice. For Plato, prudence is the wisdom to discern how to work for justice. Temperance is the ability to order passion and energy for the pursuit of good. Courage is steadfastness in the pursuit of justice, especially in the face of threat. Justice, the supreme virtue, is served by these other three. Together, these four are the cardinal virtues. Aristotle even manages a brief poetic outburst in praise of justice, which, he says, 'is often regarded as the sovereign virtue, and "neither evening nor morning star is such a wonder". We express it in a proverb, In justice is summed up the whole of virtue.'[2]

St Thomas Aquinas offers a similar view of the cardinal virtues. But for him, as for St Paul, they are subject to the great theological virtues of faith, hope and love; and the greatest of these is love. 'Owe no-one anything' wrote St Paul 'except to love one another, for love is the fulfilling of the law.'[3] The highest requirement of the law is justice, and justice is fulfilled through love. 'There are no moral laws that are absolute,' wrote William Temple, 'except the law that you should love your neighbour as you love yourself.'[4]

Justice regulates, love creates. Justice expresses right and wrong, love is concerned not simply with right and wrong, but with good and bad. Justice is love in action, but justice is part, not the whole, of righteous love.

The phrase, 'righteous love' is easy to use, but it needs some substantial content. Otherwise both justice and love may degenerate into subjective feelings, and decisions about life and death, and everything in between, will be made on the basis of what individuals happen to think is the most loving thing to do. Many people have reflected profoundly on the nature and the meaning of righteous love, among them St Augustine. In doing so he coined a memorable but exposed phrase, a phrase open to repeated misunderstanding.

'LOVE, AND DO WHAT YOU WILL'

In the most famous sermon he ever preached, St Augustine asked this strange question: 'Christ was delivered up by the Father, and delivered up by Judas: is there no seeming likeness between these two acts? Judas is a betrayer; then is God too a betrayer?' St Augustine answers his question in the phrase for which the sermon is so famous: 'Love, and do what you will.'[5] That phrase is now quoted frequently to justify the sentiment that 'Love changes everything', that 'all you need is love'. Superficially, the sermon itself, and its context, do lend some support to this. But only superficially.

St Augustine was a bishop of the Church in Africa, in the fifth century, at a time when the Church was deeply and terribly divided. The divisions did not remain at the level of civilized argument, in which St Augustine invariably presented the stronger case. They were also the cause of hatred and violence. Eventually, and with the greatest reluctance, St Augustine had to accept that there was no alternative to the use of force. The Roman Empire, so recently transformed from being the Church's persecutor to serving as its patron, declared the schism unlawful, and used force – a system of very heavy fines, sometimes even physical violence – to end the divisions.

In the winter of the year 414, the cathedral in Hippo was crowded as people listened to their Bishop Augustine delivering a series of homilies on St John's gospel. At Eastertide in the year 415, he interrupted his work on the gospel to deliver ten homilies on the first letter of John. The seventh homily ends with 'a word on that schism which violators of charity have brought about', though it is a sturdy word: 'Back, brigands! Back, usurpers of Christ's estate!' This is the context in which 'love and do what you will' was first spoken.

To the question, 'What makes the difference between the Father delivering up the son, the son delivering up himself, and Judas the disciple delivering up his master?' St Augustine answers: 'In that Father and son did it in charity, Judas in treachery. You see the point we are making,' he continues. 'Some actions seem harsh or savage, but are performed for our discipline at the dictate of charity. Thus a short and simple precept is given you once for all: love, and do what you will. Whether you keep silent, keep silence in love; whether you exclaim, exclaim in love; whether you correct, correct in love; whether you forbear, forbear in love. Let love's root be within you, and from that root nothing but good can spring.'

It was entirely clear to St Augustine that if the use of the Imperial power had been inspired by hatred or revenge, it would have been wrong. Because it was done in a spirit of unalterable love, it was not thereby made right, but it was, in the end, good. Detached from St Augustine's rigorous understanding of both love and justice, his 'short and simple precept' becomes an excuse for disguising even the most dubious actions with a coating of sugary love. But even in its context, 'love and do what you will' is a tragic defence of force in the service of love, an epitaph written on the gravestone of ideals by the uneasy conscience of a troubled man. Far from being a simple guide to good behaviour, St Augustine's most famous phrase requires that love be defined with great clarity.

DIRECT AND SIMPLE QUESTIONS

Two ways of thinking about justice often fail at this precise point. Both need some careful exploration because both are popular, possibly because they ask such simple and direct questions. One asks, What is the most useful thing to do? The other asks, What is the most loving thing to do? Both may be illustrated by another tragic case different from, though parallel to, that of Mrs Boyes.

Anthony Bland was a victim of the Hillsborough disaster, when ninety-five people died at the Sheffield Wednesday football ground. His chest was crushed, his brain deprived of oxygen, but he did not die. He was left in what is known as a persistent vegetative state, incapable of knowing anyone or of feeling anything. He was kept alive only by sustained medical treatment and by artificial feeding. In a sense, he was a victim not only of the original disaster, but also of medical science. A few years ago, he would have died fairly quickly as a result of his injuries.

His parents and doctors cared for him with great skill and devotion, and were prepared to do so indefinitely. But as they sat by his bedside day after day, knowing their son could never respond to them ever again, they were bound to ask hard questions: What is the right thing to do? What is the most useful thing to do? What is the most loving thing to do? And a fourth question, which was of particular concern to the doctors, What is it lawful for us to do?

WHAT IS LAWFUL?

The answer to the last question was provided by the courts on 4 February 1993. Five judges decided unanimously that it would not be lawful for doctors to end his life deliberately, but that the doctors would be acting within the law if they stopped feeding Tony Bland artificially, and allowed him to die.

Lord Browne Wilkinson wondered how it could be lawful to allow a patient to die slowly though painlessly from lack of food, but unlawful to end his life deliberately by lethal injection. The method may be different, but the motive is the same, the intention is the same, and the result is the same. To suggest that there is a significant difference between making something happen (by fatal injection) and allowing something to happen (by withdrawing food) is a difficult distinction morally. His Lordship could find no moral justification for the distinction, even though it is, he said, undoubtedly the law.

THE RIGHT THING TO DO?

The legal position may have been relatively clear, but the moral questions were, and still are, immensely difficult. The difference between Anthony Bland and Lilian Boyes was that she actively wanted to die, and was able to make her wishes known. Tony Bland was aware of nothing. He did not know that he was being kept alive by medical treatment, and he could not even say whether he wanted it to continue. One of the Law Lords pointed out that Anthony Bland had no 'best interests'. He felt nothing and knew nothing. 'The distressing truth which must not be shirked,' said Lord Mustill, 'is he has no best interests of any kind.'[6]

For some people, that made the question – What is the right thing to do? – a little easier. A person who is aware of nothing, they argued, and who can never relate to anyone again as a person, is no longer a person. Without medical intervention he would have died, and it would therefore be right to bring that intervention to an end. Others argued that Tony Bland was a severely disabled person, no different from other severely disabled people needing constant medical care in hospitals and homes. The right thing therefore would be to continue that care.

When people ask what is the right thing to do, there is sometimes a serious lack of clarity in the question. It may mean what is the best thing to do; or the most loving; or the most useful. Right, for the purposes of this discussion, is used in the strict sense which the word sometimes has in moral philosophy. It means conforming to a given standard.

If it had been agreed that Anthony Bland was no longer a person, and therefore need no longer be treated equally with other people, the right course of action would have been clear. But it was not agreed. If it had been agreed that life is absolutely sacred, then it would have been wrong to end his life by either deliberate action or deliberate inaction. Again the right course would have been clear. But the court took the view, for reasons we have considered in relation to Mrs Boyes, that the principle of the sanctity of life is not absolute. With no agreed moral standard, there could be no clear answer to the question 'What is the right thing to do?' The judges therefore did what a great many people now do. They concentrated on the consequences of various possible courses of action and asked: 'What will be of most benefit?'

THE MOST USEFUL THING TO DO?

This way of thinking about justice has a name and a story. The name is utilitarianism. The story is of social reformers like Bentham and Mill in the eighteenth and nineteenth centuries, and a long line of distinguished and influential successors. The neatest definition of utilitarianism is provided by Dame Mary Warnock in her Introduction to the 1984 Report of the Committee of Inquiry on Human Fertilization and Embryology: 'The principle of utility lays down, as the foundation of morality, that an act is right if it benefits more people than it harms, wrong if the balance is the other way.'[7]

Mary Warnock holds that this is neither an adequate nor a particularly helpful way in which to make moral decisions; but it is arguable that some of the conclusions of her report are in fact based on a simple utilitarian calculus. The Inquiry recommended, for example, that research on human embryos up to fourteen days old should be permitted, a recommendation which was eventually accepted by Parliament in 1990. That recommendation was based on the view that in its very early stages the human embryo, though undoubtedly human, is a 'few cells, and it would be absurd to place its welfare on an equal footing with that of other humans who might benefit from research'.[8] Here again is the word benefit, which looms so large in the case of Anthony Bland.

Lord Browne-Wilkinson said in his judgement that the correct question to be decided was whether it was in Anthony Bland's best interests to continue invasive medical care; and he concluded that there was no 'affirmative benefit' in doing so. But what does benefit mean here? The classic definition of utilitarianism was provided by J. S. Mill who wrote that 'Utility, or the Greatest Happiness Principle, holds that actions are right in proportion as they tend to promote happiness, wrong as they tend to produce the reverse of happiness. By happiness is intended pleasure, and the absence of pain; by unhappiness, pain, and the privation of pleasure.'[9]

For all its apparent simplicity and effectiveness, this principle is open to two grave objections. It depends heavily on a clear understanding of pain and pleasure, and such definitions have never been provided. Mill suggested that the ultimate end of human beings is nobility of character, and an existence free, so far as possible, from pain, 'and as rich as possible in enjoyment, both in point of quantity and quality'. Bach or the Beatles, Mozart or Madonna: who is to decide what is quantity or quality? 'Those', said Mill, 'best furnished with the means of comparison.' It is not a particularly adequate definition of happiness, though it is, of course, fatal to someone like Anthony Bland, who could appreciate nothing and had no quality of life. But the question – What is the most useful thing to do? What will bring most benefit? – is not as simple as it may seem. The calculation of consequences may prove impossibly difficult.

It is one thing to ask whether a course of action is in the best interests of just one person, quite another to estimate the benefit and harm to family and friends and society, including the elderly people described so vividly by Elizabeth Jennings. To conclude that there would be greater benefit and least harm to Anthony Bland from withdrawing treatment is relatively simple; far more difficult to calculate the best interests of his family, of the nursing staff, and of society at large.

The most disturbing possibility in the conclusion reached by the court is that the decision to end Anthony Bland's life was made, not in his interests, but in the interests of other people. It is at this point that the utilitarian calculus is most vulnerable. It aims at happiness for the greatest number of people; but because it fails to define happiness, and has no firm hold on righteous love, it can too easily slide down into injustice and misery for a significant minority. For Bentham and Mill, the human rights of individuals were less significant than the general happiness of the majority of people.

The consequences of using the utilitarian calculus in political judgements will be considered further in the next chapter. Our concern here is with those ways of making moral decisions which fail to hold firmly to both justice and love; and utilitarianism is not the only example of such failure.

THE MOST LOVING THING?

There was a popular movement in the 1960s associated with Joseph Fletcher in America and John Robinson in Britain which advocated a morality for people 'come of age'. It was, and still is, known as Situation Ethics. It holds that the one essential question to be asked in every situation is : 'What is the most loving thing to do?' The rules, the moral standards and the teachings of past generations have no absolute nor any intrinsic validity. They are the deposits placed in the Bank of Human Experience. Anyone can draw upon those deposits freely. They could be useful. But the only valid question to be asked is, what is the most loving thing to do now, in this particular situation? 'Even the most revered principles', says Joseph Fletcher 'may be thrown aside if they conflict in any concrete situation with love.'[10]

Only love, and nothing but love, is good in itself. Love wills what is good, regardless of personal likes and dislikes. Love must decide, not by applying rules but by discovering the most loving thing to do in each different situation. Only the consequences can justify the means, and if the end is love, then the end will be justice in action, because justice is love distributed. The only question to be asked by Anthony Bland's parents and doctors is, therefore, what is the most loving thing to do, here, now, in this situation?

It is not difficult to see why John Robinson wrote, in the distant days of the 1960s, in *Honest to God*, that this 'is the only ethic for "man come of age"'.[11] To obey rules is relatively easy and demands no special insight or maturity. Given sufficiently severe sanctions or the promise of adequate reward, a child can do it. But it requires personal responsibility and some courage to treat all the traditions and rules of the past as mere illustrations, and to rely only on love. No wonder Pope Pius XII tried to nip such thinking in the bud when he condemned it, as early as 1952, as individualistic and subjective, an attempt to justify decisions which are in opposition to the natural law and the revealed will of God. He was particularly concerned about the suggestion that right and wrong and good and bad may not be precisely the same.

For Bishop Robinson, it was rather more than a suggestion. 'Nothing can of itself always be labelled as "wrong"', he wrote.[12] Divorce may not be right, but in some circumstances it may be good.

RIGHT OR WRONG, GOOD OR BAD

A morality rooted in absolute moral laws will generally be clear and straightforward about what is right and wrong. People will know where they are. It will set standards, talk about duty, and indicate as clearly as possible what you ought to do. It will say, for example, that you must always speak the truth; and if there are any exceptions, they will be clearly defined. You may tell a lie only if doing so will save an innocent life.

A morality of good and bad requires a clear, well-defined understanding of what is good. It depends heavily on the clarity with which positive ideals are set out. Actions will be judged good if they help to achieve those ideals, bad if they do not. Its greatest risk is that it will degenerate into competing ideas of what is good. Objective standards will disintegrate. Justice will become a matter of personal opinion. Our understanding of what is good will be determined by the devices and desires of our own hearts. A morality of good and bad may be confused and confusing. It is risky. People have been crucified because they have argued for what is good, rather than for what is generally considered right.

The Roman Catholic Church teaches clearly that the use

of artificial means of birth regulation is always wrong. The Papal Encyclical, *Veritatis Splendor*, published in 1993, states that morality is based on the will of God, and is not determined by what people want, nor by what they may consider good, but by what is right. It admits no distinction between right and good. The will of God, revealed in the natural law and in the tradition of the Church, tells that sexual relations between men and women are primarily for the purpose of reproduction, and must always be open to that possibility. Therefore artificial means of regulating reproduction must always be wrong.

Large numbers of Roman Catholics, possibly now a majority, consider that the use of contraceptives is good. It gives the freedom to enjoy sexual relations while at the same time controlling the size of the family. It would, they argue, be bad, destructively and irresponsibly bad, not to control the increase in the world's population. Therefore, whether it is right or not, the use of artificial means of birth regulation is good.

Slowly a belief is growing in the Roman Catholic Church that the traditional understanding of what is natural is incomplete, and that sexual relations are primarily for the expression of love; in which case, what is good and what is right may eventually be recognized as being the same.

EXCELLENCE

A satisfactory morality will always try to combine the right and the good, and will then devise ways of coping when the good and the right do not coincide. The Greek thinkers combined good and right in the idea of excellence; though they were more concerned with what is good than with what is right. The Greek word which we translate as virtue means simply excellence. Excellence is the highest idea of the good. It is the wholeness, the integrity of human life lived in accordance with the highest ideals. The good is eternal reality, ultimately unknowable, yet drawing the highest and purest longings of human beings into itself.

St Paul's classical education must have included such thinking, though there are few references to excellence in his writing. The best known is in his letter to the Philippians – 'Whatever is true, whatever is honourable, whatever is just, whatever is pure, whatever is lovely, whatever is gracious, if there is any excellence, if there is anything worthy of praise, think about these things' (Philippians 4:8). His reference to excellence is almost casual – 'if there's anything in this Greek idea . . .'

For St Paul, the ideal of excellence is embodied and transformed in the life of Jesus. When he urges Christians towards the goal of wholeness, completeness in faith and in the knowledge of God, the ideal is measured by nothing less than the stature of Christ himself. But few things were more confusing to the Pharisees, or more liberating to the people, than the fact that Jesus chose what he considered to be the good, rather than abiding by current understandings of right.

The long controversy about the Sabbath is given great prominence in the gospels because it focuses this crucial question. Observation of the Sabbath was a matter of right and wrong. Its origins lay in the ten commandments, which provided absolute moral authority. Detailed rules regulated every conceivable action which might be contemplated. When Jesus plucked ears of corn on the Sabbath, it was an apparently trivial but highly controversial action. The Pharisees were quick to point out that he was departing from the path of right and wrong. 'It is not lawful,' they said. Jesus justifies his action by appealing to the example of David, who took bread on the Sabbath because he and his men needed it, and because it was good for them to do so. 'The Sabbath is made for man,' Jesus said, 'not man for the Sabbath.'[13]

What is ultimately for the good of human beings may be even more important than strict obedience to right and wrong. The row over the Sabbath, so fully and carefully recorded in the gospels, is quite literally crucial. The path Jesus chose led ultimately to the Cross. But the disagreement was caused, not as the Pharisees thought, because Jesus rejected the commandments of God, but because he was angered by the perversion of righteous love into a code of rules. Nor was he content merely to release people from the tyranny of absolute moral laws. Nor even to revive the heart and spirit of Jewish faith which was suffocating under layers of rules. He lived so fully in the spirit of righteous love that he gave new meaning to both justice and love.

THE POWER OF LOVE

The love which Jesus lived is the love which St Paul describes so eloquently in 1 Corinthians 13. It is gentle and understanding, yet capable of devastating severity. It is patient and kind, yet relentless and demanding in pursuit of the highest good. It is hopeful and realistic.

In the Garden of Gethsemane, love is fearful and courageous. Before the Sanhedrin, love is truthful. Before Pilate and Herod, love is silent. Under the mocking and the scourging, love is ridiculed and abused; and as the nails are driven through flesh into wood, love screams, and then forgives those who don't know what they are doing. In long agony on the cross, love is rejected, forsaken; despairs; and then, at the last, revives.

Love, on the Cross, is uncalculating generosity, self-giving without limit, with neither hope nor expectation of any reward. Love is strong, but vulnerable; wise, and absurdly foolish; rational, but so unconfined by reason as to be gloriously irrational. Love is the purest power, a power which recognizes that nothing purely good can ever be achieved by force. Love is the power which dies in weakness. There is no security in love. Love is betrayed or ignored, laughed at and abused, tormented and crucified. 'Love bears all things, believes all things, hopes all things, endures all things. Love never ends.'

TO SPEAK ABOUT THE UNSPEAKABLE

What then are we to say about the Holocaust? It is difficult enough, though it is possible, to see the binding of Isaac as the will of God and the command of righteous love. It is hard, though possible, to see the action of a loving and righteous God in the suffering and death of Christ. But can we say anything at all about the Six Million?

To think about it, to try to enter into the experience of those who died or of those who survived is impossibly hard. Even to attempt it is to enter a terrible darkness. How can anyone think or speak about the unspeakable? But to remain silent about the worst injustice in the life of humanity, especially in a book about justice, is impossible too. 'Through the experience of the death camps,' writes Marc Ellis, 'an innocence that cannot be recovered is lost.

The world has changed, and so has faith.' For some, Christians as well as Jews, 'the omnipotent, benevolent God of history is shown to be a farce . . . God indeed is a culpable figure.'[14]

It is understandable that Arab children in Israel today know little about the Holocaust, and that teaching about it is confined to one short history lesson. It is intolerable that British and American children are largely ignorant of the most basic facts. If the various surveys are correct, they are doubtful about whether such a thing could possibly have happened.

The various scholarly attempts to discredit the evidence, to pretend that it never happened, that 'the chimneys were bakeries', is an obscenity. Are the Jews who died to be put to death a third time? They were killed in the gas chambers, the first death. Their bodies were burned, to obliterate them, the second death. Are they now to die again, the remembrance of them extinguished in the slow, damp fires of forgetfulness?

Lieb Langfuss, a rabbinic judge, is one of those many hundreds who wrote in order to describe what was happening, and who hid their words before they died, hoping against hope that we would find them, and know, and remember.

'We witnessed the arrival of transports from Bendin and Sosnowiec,' wrote Langfuss. 'An elderly rabbi was among them. They came from nearby towns, and they knew what was awaiting them. They knew. And the rabbi entered the undressing room, and suddenly he began to dance and to sing all alone. And the others said nothing and he sang and he danced for a long time and then he died for *kiddush ha-shem*, for the sanctification of God's name.'[15]

Attempts to explain, attempts to excuse or to justify the

Holocaust in any way, all fail. The most humane, the most positive, the best-intentioned attempts, they all fail. The most positive is this: that out of the ashes, out of the guilt, the horror and the sympathy of the Western world, the State of Israel was born. Not only the survivors, but all Jews have a homeland, a place to be, at last. Without the Six Million, it might never have happened.

Israel is one thing, a small but welcome consolation for the Jewish people. The State of Israel, as some kind of justification for the deaths of the Six Million, is something else altogether. The trial of Eichmann was held in Israel, and a man who testified in that trial was asked if he could now, at some distance in time, find any meaning in Auschwitz. 'I hope I never do,' he replied. 'To understand would be even worse than not to understand it.'

THE SILENCE OF DEATH

There is no meaning in the Holocaust, only death and silence. Of course there are the 'explanations'. It was claimed for centuries that the Jews deserved to be harried and persecuted as the killers of Christ. The seeds of that persecution were sown in St John's gospel, and they have been harvested all through the centuries. But generations of persecuted Jews, and finally (or maybe not finally) six million for one man? What kind of justice, what kind of demon God is this, that people will advance such monstrous 'explanations'?

Those centuries when hatred of the Jews was encouraged and allowed in supposedly Christian countries, and the failure of nearly all the churches to do anything at all to prevent the Holocaust, means that Christians have to face the dreadful problem of complicity in the death of the Six Million. 'If I want to understand,' writes Elie Wiesel, 'and never will, why my people turned into victims, into perfect victims, somebody will have to understand, or try to understand why all the killers were Christians, bad Christians surely, but Christians.'[16] 'What does it mean', asks another Jew, Marc Ellis, 'to be a Christian when Christian understandings and actions issued in the death camps?'[17]

For some of the Jews themselves, there is only one 'explanation' that has any credibility, and even that is inadequate. It is that God should not be held responsible for the evil done by human beings. In 1980, Robert Brenner published the results of a detailed and careful study of *The Faith and Doubt of Holocaust Survivors*. Detailed letters sent to one thousand Israeli survivors elicited over seven hundred replies. One hundred were interviewed personally, the rest by further correspondence. The study is filled not merely with statistics, but with the comments of the survivors.

One question in the study was this: 'With regard to the destruction of the Six Million, which one of these responses is the most acceptable to you?

a. It is inappropriate to blame God for the acts of man
b. It is not for us to judge the ways of God
c. God was unable to prevent the destruction
d. The Holocaust was the will of God
e. Nothing can excuse God for not having saved them.'[18]

A quarter of the people could not respond to the question because of the way it was framed. Of those who were able to respond, the clearest and strongest preference, 34%, was for answer (b), that it is not for us to judge the ways of God. 27% chose not to blame God for the acts of man (a). 25% thought nothing could excuse God for not having saved them (e). 9% considered the Holocaust to be the will of God (d) and still less that God was unable to prevent it (c).

To say that it is not for us to judge God's ways is not an attempt to explain what happened. It is an act of faith. One in four of the survivors remained believers in a personal God, though not all chose this reply. Of those who did, one wrote: 'My faith in God was not undermined in the least. It just never occurred to me to associate the calamity we were experiencing with God, to blame him, or to believe in him less or to cease believing in him at all because he didn't come to our aid.'[19]

To say that it is not right to blame God for the acts of men is an explanation favoured by a substantial number of survivors. It is the only explanation which has any credibility. 'Confined within the barbed wire of Auschwitz,' writes another, 'I understood to separate the wicked deeds of men from the workings of the entire universe. The system of the world, and the idea behind its functioning is God. I have always believed that. I never believed God to be a kindly old man with a beard watching out for the welfare of each and every person. And within the workings of the world, man can commit atrocities and murder or refrain from atrocities and murder. He is free to choose. God is not a puppeteer pulling the strings and making men dance. God doesn't act to stop murder.'[20]

That explanation is plausible only because it contains important truth about human freedom and responsibility. But it is a truth which satisfies only a small proportion of people. A far larger number were puzzled, angry, even destroyed, by the silence of God. Of those who clung to belief, in spite of the calamity, many thought that nothing could excuse the fact that God failed to prevent it. An even larger number, a quarter of the 700, did not believe in God at all. For them, all five of the suggested answers were unsatisfactory because all five included the word God. Some had no faith before the Holocaust. Others ceased to believe because of it.

A hesitant, uncertain atheist quickly abandoned all uncertainty. 'Five minutes of seeing dead bodies scattered along the road; corpses lying in grotesque formations; heaps of the dead and dying, by the hundreds – five minutes and I knew I could never believe in a God who'd not prevent this.'[21]

Another, a strong believer before, sums up: 'When an entire people, a good people who never were evil, prayed for a good purpose: their deliverance from destruction by an evil people, and for whatever reason God turned away and refused to answer their sincere and genuine prayers, when good people, good prayers for good purposes go unanswered, the only conclusion I can arrive at is that God does not exist.'[22]

ARGUMENT AND LAMENT

The Jewish people have always combined the faith of Abraham, that the judge of all the earth will do what is just, with an unrivalled capacity for argument and lament. The writer of one of the Psalms puts a suggestion to God somewhat wistfully, almost as an afterthought: 'In your goodness, kill off my enemies.' Other Psalms are more direct – 'Let God arise and let his enemies be scattered': more explicit – 'Happy is he who repays you for what you have done to us, who takes your babies and smashes them against the rocks': more intense – 'O Lord my defender, I call to you. Listen to my cry! If you do not answer me, I will be among those who go down to the pit.'

God did not answer at Auschwitz, or Dachau, or Treblinka. The anguished screams of God's murdered people were met with a deadly silence which leaves questions echoing still amongst the bones, the ashes and the memorials. After the Holocaust, after Hiroshima, in a world where children are abused and the hungry are not filled with anything, let alone the good things promised long ago in the Magnificat, Abraham's ancient question has great urgency: 'Shall not the judge of all the earth do what is just?'

For Elie Wiesel, a survivor whose writing has done so much to serve the remembrance of those who died and the healing of those who survived, it is the silence of God that is so terrible. No justification, no explanation, nothing can excuse this awful silence. But it is Elie Wiesel's own questions which begin to penetrate that silent and dreadful darkness.

The first of his many books is a personal account of his own experience in the death camps. It is called *Night*. He was taken to one of the camps at the age of fifteen. He was a pious, Hasidic Jew, but on the first day, his faith was consumed in the flames and the smoke billowing out of a long trench in which the bodies of young children were being burned. 'Never shall I forget that smoke. Never shall I forget those flames, which consumed my faith for ever. Never shall I forget those moments which murdered my God and my soul and turned my dreams to dust.'[23]

The book includes what is now a well-known and dreadful account of the execution of a child. It is often quoted because it can be made to speak so clearly of the suffering of God. But it is also used to indicate the faith of survivors such as Wiesel, and that may do less than justice to the depth of his questioning.

Rabbi Dan Cohn-Sherbok, who knows that the Holocaust poses the most serious and haunting religious question ever, tells us that in this story, 'Elie Wiesel has provided an answer.'[24] The Christian theologian Jurgen Moltmann uses the story for the same purpose.[25] But it is not so. Neither Jews nor Christians should lay claim to Wiesel's experience too readily.

In 1979, Wiesel wrote a play called *The Trial of God*, which is based on a personal experience in the death camps: 'Inside the kingdom of night, I witnessed a strange trial. Three rabbis – all erudite and pious men – decided one winter evening to indict God for allowing his children to be massacred. I remember: I was there and I felt like crying. But there, nobody cried.'[26]

THE TRIAL OF GOD

In *The Trial of God*, the prosecutor spells out the charges: 'I accuse him of hostility, cruelty and indifference. Either he dislikes his chosen people or he doesn't care about them. But then, why has he chosen us? Why not someone else for a change? Either he knows what's happening to us, or he doesn't wish to know. In both cases he is . . . he is . . . guilty (*Pause. Loud and clear*) Yes, Guilty!'[27]

The defence argued that 'Men and women and children were massacred by other men. Why implicate their Father in Heaven?', a defence which echoes Brenner's survey. But the trial does not come to an end. The participants are destroyed before they can reach a verdict. The play ends with 'deafening and murderous roars'. In the silence of death which follows, the questions are left hanging.

The well-known account which Wiesel gives in his book *Night*, which some take to be 'an answer', is this. Along with everyone else in the camp, he is forced to watch a dreadful, harrowing execution, Golgotha in a death camp called Buna. There were three victims, two adults and a young boy; three chairs, three nooses.

' "Long live liberty!" cried the two adults. But the child was silent. "Where is God? Where is he?" someone behind me asked. At a sign from the head of the camp, the three chairs tipped over. Total silence throughout the camp. On the horizon, the sun was setting. Then the march past began. The two adults were no longer alive. But the third rope was still moving. For more than half an hour, the child stayed there, struggling between life and death, dying in slow agony. Behind me I heard the same man asking, "Where is God now ?" And I heard a voice within me answer him: "Where is he? Here he is – he is hanging here, on this gallows." '[28]

The same dreadul silence echoed around Golgotha. 'When the sixth hour came, there was darkness over all the land until the ninth hour. And at the ninth hour, Jesus cried out in a loud voice, "Eloi, Eloi, lama sabachthani?" which means, "My God, my God, why did you forsake me?" When some of those who stood by heard this, they said, "Listen, he is calling Elijah." Someone ran and soaked a sponge in vinegar and, putting it on a reed, gave it to him to drink saying, "Wait! And see if Elijah will come to take him down." But Jesus gave a loud cry and breathed his last.'[29]

Where is God when the rope is finally still, when Jesus hangs dead on the Cross? Where is God now, the God of Abraham and Isaac, the God of Hitler and Wiesel, the God and Father of our Lord Jesus Christ? The God of Calvary and Auschwitz may be victim; or executioner; or spectator; or mad; or participant. Which? The slow death of a child, and the desolate agony of Christ, mean that all those five possibilities must be taken seriously.

An act of power, of divinely imposed justice, would have stopped the Holocaust, just as it would also have stopped the Crucifixion. 'Wait! And see whether Elijah will come and take him down.' Moslems believe that Jesus did not die on the Cross: 'they did not kill him, nor did they crucify him,' says the Qur'an, 'but they thought they did. God lifted him up to Him; God is mighty and wise.'[30] For Moslems, the sovereignty of the God of justice demands that history is rewritten in the Qur'an, just as justice and the weight of horror require for some people that the scale and the reality of the Holocaust be denied.

But if God is love, if love is the ultimate reality, then the sovereignty of justice cannot be imposed by force without subverting love. The love which is pure and self-giving, the love which creates, cannot rule by force. It is a love which is vulnerable, a love which may be crucified, or gassed, or burned in the fires of evil.

The price of love is vulnerability to great evil. The risk and the hope of love creates the possibility of love returned, in relationships freely chosen. The creative act of God is an act of such pure and self-giving love that human beings are given the one and only absolute and unconditional freedom, the freedom to be. This is, perhaps, in part, what it means to be created in the image of God. It is this creative love of God which is ultimately responsible for all that is, for Abraham and Isaac, for Calvary, for Belsen and for Buna. It is the love of the God who shares in the whole of life, who is both victim and executioner, priest and sacrifice, justice and love, the God who lives the divine madness of absolute love.

Some years after the liberation, when Elie Wiesel was working as a young journalist, he went to interview the writer, François Mauriac. In his introduction to Wiesel's book, *Night*, Mauriac wrote this:

'I, who believe that God is love, what answer could I give my young questioner, whose dark eyes still held the reflection of that angelic sadness which had appeared one day upon the face of the hanged child? What did I say to him? Did I affirm that the stumbling block to his faith was the cornerstone of mine, and that the conformity between the Cross and the suffering of human beings was in my eyes the key to that impenetrable mystery whereon the faith of his childhood had perished? This is what I should have told this Jewish child. But I could only embrace him, weeping.'[31]

FOUR

WORKING FOR JUSTICE

On 2 August 1990 the armies of Iraq moved into Kuwait, crushed opposition, and took control of the country. That act of aggression unleashed a torrent of outrage, of analysis and of idealism. The injustice was strongly condemned on all sides. Hopes were voiced of a new world order, in which the nations would act together to restrain, punish and eliminate such aggression. Within a remarkably short time, Desert Shield was in place, to prevent the tentacles of evil from reaching out even further. By the end of 2 August, the UN Security Council had passed Resolution 660, condemning the invasion and demanding Iraq's immediate and unconditional withdrawal.

There was then a brief period of assessment and analysis. Politicians, retired generals, church people, journalists, all had their say. The mountain of words grew daily. The Security Council passed eight more resolutions by the end of September.[1] Out of it all, two serious possibilities for action emerged: either the continuation and increase of sanctions coupled with international pressure and negotiation for a just solution; or the use of overwhelming force to liberate Kuwait. Both courses of action were held by different people, with equal passion, to be right. Both were based on differing interpretations of what has come to be known as 'Just War Theory'. It is an unfortunate title for a necessary attempt to think clearly about war. In fact, a 'just war' is never possible, because war is always and inevitably unjust, in its causes, its methods and its results.

CAUSES, METHODS AND RESULTS

The cause of the Gulf War was not a simple case of evil aggression. Justice was not on one side only. For years,

Britain and America supported Saddam Hussein and Iraq in the war against Iran. It served Western interests to do so. It was a different matter when Saddam Hussein attacked Western interests by annexing Kuwait, and by threatening further advances into Saudi Arabia, which would have given Iraq a stranglehold on one quarter of the world's oil production.

There may not have been much justice in Iraq's invasion of Kuwait, but there was some. It was obscured when Western politicians, aided by the media, quickly began the process of demonizing Saddam Hussein. The *Los Angeles Times* caught the public mood in America and Britain in an editorial published the morning after the invasion: 'The aggression was undisguised, the greed was naked, the operation was swift, vengeful and effective. In just a few hours, Iraq's dictator, Saddam Hussein, wolfed down all of Kuwait and sat back to gloat.'[2]

Reports, which were later proved to be wrong, were quickly in circulation, such as the removal of babies from incubators in a hospital in Kuwait, so that the equipment could be transferred to Iraq. Reports of other atrocities committed against the people of Kuwait were given wide circulation. The fact that there was a genuine and long-standing dispute over the border between Iraq and Kuwait, and over side-drilling by Kuwait into Iraqi oil fields, was largely ignored. So too was the economic warfare against Iraq in which Kuwait had long been engaged, by lowering the price of oil and so attempting to ruin Iraq's economy. Iraq gave clear warning that a resort to armed retaliation was their only option. Western nations responded with strangely ambiguous signals, an ambiguity which was 'a failure in policy, diplomacy and intelligence.'[3]

If the causes of the war were a mixture of justice and

injustice, so too, inevitably, were the methods, on both sides. Saddam Hussein's desperate attempt to involve other Arab nations, by firing missiles at Israel, was a dreadful evil. So too was Iraq's treatment of prisoners of war. The attempt to impose rules on the conduct of war is an attempt to maintain at least a crust of civilization over the erupting horrors of destruction and death. It is particularly the treatment of prisoners, those most vulnerable casualties of war, which indicates what remains of civilization.

Iraq's treatment of the very first prisoners, the pilots of Tornado aircraft, was like a jagged hole in that thin crust, which brought with it the danger that the conflict would sink deeper into barbarism. But again the evil was not on one side only. The determination of the Allied forces to end the war swiftly, with as few Allied casualties as possible, was clearly right; but it resulted in Iraqi soldiers being buried alive in their trenches, which were filled in by Allied tanks with specially fitted blades. And it ended with that appalling slaughter which left the Basra Road littered with the charred bodies of Iraqi soldiers, faces melted into nightmarish grins.

The results of the war were no less ambiguous than its causes and its methods. Kuwait was 'liberated', though that meant in practice that it was handed back to its corrupt ruling family. The military power of Iraq was decimated, and in particular, its capacity to produce nuclear weapons was reduced if not eliminated, though only with the greatest difficulty. But Saddam Hussein remained in power, and continued to plague the Kurds and the Marsh Arabs. Hopes of a new world order, inspired by the large coalition of nations mobilized under the authority of the United Nations, were diminished when many Arab and Third World countries condemned the new order as the hijacking of the United Nations by Western interests

Whether a more just order would have emerged from the continued imposition of sanctions, coupled with intensive diplomatic negotiation, can never be known; because for a variety of reasons, some good, some bad, Desert Shield was turned into Desert Storm. The Gulf War was fought and decisively won by the Allied Forces. Some justified the war, and its inevitable and terrible consequences, on the grounds that all the possible alternatives would have resulted in continuing and growing injustice. Others concluded that the attempt to create justice by force had only made a bad situation worse. War is always a descent into barbarism. It is evil. To dignify it as 'just' when its causes, methods and results are always and inevitably unjust is to abuse language. War can only be justified because the best possible estimate of all the available alternatives indicates that not to go to war would be even more unjust.

A JUST WAR – IN THEORY

What is known as the doctrine of the just war is an attempt to think coherently about the circumstances in which war might be the lesser of two evils; and because human beings have fought each other for a long time, such thinking has a long history. There are two parallel traditions which run into each other at many points, one based primarily on rational thought, the other on revelation and religious experience. Those differing ways of thinking resulted in the three main views which were held, not only at the time of the Gulf War, but also during the First and the Second World Wars.

The pacifist view is that war is always wrong. There are no circumstances in which the use of violence can be justified. For some people, the teaching of Jesus in this matter is clear and decisive. For others, Jesus sets out ideals which are not always possible in an evil world. For them, the doctrine of the just war is an attempt to apply Biblical and religious insights in the fight against evil. Some concluded that in the particular circumstances of Iraq's invasion of Kuwait, war was justified. Others came to a different conclusion.

In the early part of its life, the dominant view in the Church was that of the pacifists. Soldiers were refused baptism while they remained in the army. War was held to be wrong, always, and in all circumstances, and contrary to the spirit and the teaching of Christ, who refused all temptation to resort to force, even in the face of suffering and death on a cross. It may be that the early Church was right, and that in the earliest days, it held firm to the clarity of Jesus' teaching with a purity which later was compromised. But it may equally be the case that the circumstances in those early centuries allowed the Church the freedom to remain largely pacifist, a freedom which the Church has never subsequently enjoyed. The Church was at first a small, persecuted minority, with no political power and little influence. It could not possibly resist persecution by force of arms, and had little choice but to accept suffering, as a good servant of Jesus Christ, and to interpret that endurance as obedience to an ideal.

As the Church increased in numbers and in influence, it ceased to be an enclave in which such ideals could be preserved and lived, and had to engage with the cold reality of political power. St Augustine, who first developed a coherent doctrine of the just war, is often credited (if that is the right word) with checking the pacifist inclinations of early Christian thought. But by the time St Augustine was writing, the pacifist view was no longer dominant, and his views on the legitimacy of waging war were widely accepted. What worried St Augustine was not the pacifist view, but the growing tendency amongst Christians to resort to force too readily, to accept the values and the methods of the society around them, and to support the Imperial forces of Rome in its battles against the barbarians, as if they were engaged in a holy war.

Far from providing a justification for war, St Augustine was concerned to restrict the easy resort to force. He considered war to be a tragic necessity to which the state might occasionally resort, when there was no other possible alternative, in order to check the savagery of evil forces.[4]

The pacifist view is clear and uncompromising, and requires little assessment of complex circumstances. War is always wrong, however evil or threatening the situation might be. Just war theory demands the most careful consideration of all the varying factors, particularly some estimate of whether the possible outcome of a war would be a just and lasting peace. The Gulf War provoked the traditional pacifist view, and also two diametrically opposed views on whether the war would or would not be the lesser of two evils.

The pacifist view and the doctrine of the just war are both derived from differing interpretations of the Bible and of Christian tradition. Such contradictory attitudes to the Gulf War provide one more example of the complexity of moral questions and the elusiveness of perfect justice.

WORKING FOR JUSTICE

Working for justice was never particularly easy in a society which had shared assumptions and a common faith, for even a shared faith may yield three or more opinions on what is right. It is far more complex and costly in a society which is now so diverse, and which has no agreed basis for making moral decisions.

Whatever the context, the pursuit of justice has always involved four distinct but interlocking elements: a willingness to share the experience of those who suffer injustice (sometimes called solidarity, which Marc Ellis defines as 'the movement of the heart, mind and body towards those who are suffering'[5]); a tenacious determination to work for ideals, values and principles; a careful understanding and analysis of the situation; specific policies and detailed plans for action. All four were clearly in place in the controversy about the Gulf War.

Working for justice is complex and costly. It demands ideals and compromises, principles and realism, analysis and action, experience and reflection. Exactly how these complementary, sometimes contradictory elements may be held together is a matter of continuing and important discussion.

Two views about the way in which Christians should work for justice have been influential and in some ways effective, though both are now seriously questioned. One is only relevant to societies which are influenced by Christian belief. It holds that the task of the Christian Church is to reinforce the values which hold society together. The classic statement of this view in the 1980s was a Church of England report called 'Changing Britain: Social Diversity and Moral Unity'. The report broadly concludes that British society, when compared with other countries, is 'an old, stable and successful culture', still influenced in significant ways by the Christian values and assumptions which are deeply rooted through long centuries of Christian belief and worship.[6] Like the acacia tree in the Judaean wilderness, there may be an appearance of dryness, but the roots go down thirty metres or so into unfailing sources of moisture.

Moreover it is suggested that at that depth, there is nothing distinctively Christian about basic principles. They derive from a shared understanding of what it means to be human. 'In terms of the principles by which people should live and societies order themselves,' writes John Habgood, 'Christians have little to say that could not be said by any reasonable person of goodwill.'[7] The difference lies in beliefs about sin and grace, incarnation and salvation, but these beliefs, he suggests, affect only the quality, not the outcome of public debate or the policies which should be pursued.

This is a curiously comfortable view, in which the harsher realities of British society and the disturbing demands of the Gospel are hard to recognize. Many young people in Britain and America (and not only young people) were disillusioned by the extent to which so many church leaders conformed to the spirit of the age in the debate about the Gulf War, and acquiesced so readily in the quick resort to violence which was dictated by political considerations.

FOUR STAGES

An earlier view of the Church's role in working for justice was powerfully argued by Archbishop William Temple. Along with many others, he maintained that there are four stages in working for justice. There is fundamental Christian theology, that body of unchanging truth which has been revealed. Out of this bedrock of Christian truth certain general moral principles may be derived. These in turn may lead to the formulation of desirable goals. How to achieve those goals in working policies and practical action is the final stage.

Temple for example begins with fundamental Christian belief, with God's purposes in creation and with human beings created equal in the image and likeness of God. From this theology, he draws general moral principles and suggests that the greatest possible freedom of personal choice, together with social fellowship in which people are primarily concerned to serve the interests of others, are the principles on which a just social order must be built. Temple also emphasized a principle now even more urgent, that 'the resources of the earth should be used as God's gifts to the whole human race, and used with due consideration for the needs of the present and future generations.'[8]

These principles he then turns into specific objectives: decent family housing; good education; adequate and regular income; a voice in decision-making; daily leisure, weekly rest and annual holiday; freedom of speech and worship. Temple spells out these six objectives in a little more detail and summarizes, 'The aim of a Christian social order is the fullest possible development of individual personality in the widest and deepest possible fellowship.'[9]

Exactly how all this might be achieved he discusses only in an appendix written from an entirely personal point of view. This most contentious and potentially divisive stage of the process he leaves mainly to the experts and the politicians since they have the technical knowledge and the responsibility. He is mindful of the comment made by the prime minister, Stanley Baldwin, in 1926, when the bishops attempted to intervene directly in the coal strike. 'How would the bishops like it,' asked Baldwin, 'if he referred to the Iron and Steel Federation the revision of the Athanasian Creed?'[10]

Politicians today have answered specific criticism from the Church by saying that the proper sphere of religion is either personal morality or general principle, but not detailed proposals or objections to particular policies. They would have been a little more comfortable with Temple's approach. But for all its attractiveness, there are serious questions to be put to this way of working for social justice.[11]

First, is fundamental theology best known through study and then application; or is the real truth of theology best discovered in a direct engagement with specific problems? Many would now say that the latter is the best way. The principles informing the debate about the Gulf War seemed at first to be a fixed body of doctrine. Just war theory was given its clearest and classic form by St Thomas Aquinas in the twelfth century. But principles governing warfare in the days of standing armies, pitched battles and bows and arrows could not be applied to the twentieth century without modification. The essential truth of the theology which St Thomas expressed in his day had to be learned again for this century. It was not a simple matter of applying the same truth in a different way. The truth itself had to be known afresh in a new situation.

Secondly, is it possible to know what general principles or even specific objectives really mean until their precise application is known? The debate about the Gulf War did not and could not end in vacuous generality. The situation demanded more than a statement of general principle. Something had to be done. Final decisions had to rest with elected politicians acting on the best military intelligence available. But the responsibility of the Churches did not end with statements of moral principle. The Churches also took account of all the available information and analysed it carefully; and then came to clear though differing conclusions about what specific action should be taken.

The most influential and effective reports are not those which state general principles or desirable goals and then stop short of specific proposals. That approach too often ends in vacuous generalization. It is reports which say in detail what should be done which set people thinking and which reveal what general principles really mean, reports like *The Church and the Bomb* or *Faith in the City*. It is the proposals and policies which people advocate or favour which indicate what they value most highly.

Solidarity, principles, analysis, action, all are essential in working for justice. But what all this may mean in practice is best explored in more detail by considering two different situations. The second, which we will come to later, is the conflict between Jews and Arabs in Palestine, a land so burdened with history and holiness. The first takes us back to the questions raised towards the end of the first chapter, the meaning of equality in relation to society in general and to government policy in the 1980s in particular.

A PRICE WORTH PAYING?

One of the more notorious comments made by a former British chancellor, Norman Lamont, was that three million people unemployed is 'a price worth paying' to bring down the rate of inflation. It was an unguarded remark which was widely thought by some people to have let the cat out of the bag. 'Now we know,' they said. 'The government doesn't really care about the unemployed.' As is often the case with political gaffes, both the original remark, and the interpretations put on it, were far too simplistic.

No government in its right mind wants to see large numbers of people unemployed. The debilitating effects on the individuals and their families are bad enough. Added to that are the high costs of unemployment benefits, and the increase in crime committed by bored, badly-off young people. Most serious of all for politicians, large numbers of unemployed people are unlikely to vote for a government whose policies have caused them to be out of work.

There is plenty of evidence to suggest that the government was in fact deeply and genuinely concerned about unemployment. But there was an even greater concern about inflation, and a widespread recognition that a high rate of inflation, as there was in the early 1980s, is crippling for everyone. In a speech in the Mansion House, London, in October 1985, Lamont's predecessor, Nigel Lawson, said, 'The acid test of monetary policy is its record in reducing inflation. The inflation rate is judge and jury.'[12]

Whether the inflation rate could have been reduced without an increase in unemployment remains a matter of intense debate. What actually happened is a matter of record. Reducing inflation was the major political priority. The inflation rate did come down dramatically. Unemployment increased disastrously, and remained at a high level.

Even so brief an account of a complex problem illustrates again the most persistent difficulty in any attempt to create a just society. Desirable goals are numerous, fundamental principles are in conflict with one another, choices are hard. It is usually not possible to put every important principle into practice. How then are we to decide which principles are most important, which goals we should aim at?

The quickest and easiest short cut through this maze is the one signposted by the Utilitarians. The most useful thing to do is whatever will bring most benefit to most people. That is the path along which the British chancellor scurried. Three million unemployed is regrettable, unfortunate, everything possible must be done to help them; but the bottom line remains clear. Three million unemployed is a price worth paying. Doing harm to a minority is justified if it benefits the majority.

TO SERVE THE GREATER HAPPINESS

Reformers like Mill and Bentham, who gave Utilitarianism its most extreme expression, did not intend this conclusion. Mill maintains that 'in the golden rule of Jesus of Nazareth, we read the complete spirit of the ethics of utility. To do as one would be done by and to love one's neighbour as oneself constitute the ideal perfection of Utilitarian morality'.[13] In thus suggesting that Jesus was a Utilitarian, Mill is indulging in a specious attempt to reassure those who were suspicious of his agnosticism. For despite Mill's use of the golden rule, his view requires us to love our neighbours only because to do so would serve the greater happiness.

Mill argues that 'laws and social arrangements should place the happiness of every individual as nearly as possible in harmony with the interests of the whole'.[14] No politician would disagree with that. The dream of every chancellor is full employment, low inflation, a low rate of taxation and sufficient resources for good education, health and social welfare. But the basic problem in modern social policy is that resources are limited and demands are great. Medical science becomes more successful and more expensive in equal measure. People live longer. Education, welfare, public services, all devour huge resources. It is simply not possible to do good to all people equally. Choices have to be made. The simplest solution is to do as much good as possible. A low rate of inflation is good for most people. Three million unemployed pay the price. A high standard of living is good for those who enjoy it. The economic slaves of the poorest countries help to pay the bill.

But what has happened to justice, to equality, and to human rights, if the greater good of the many can be served by violating the liberty of a few? Mill, like all the Utilitarians, has a precarious hold on human rights. So too did Caiaphas. 'It is expedient (more use),' he said, 'that one man should die for the people than that the whole nation should perish.'[15] Rights are rights if they serve the principle of utility, Mill argued. Human rights, even justice itself, are valid because they are useful. Most of the time, in most societies, the greatest good is secured by the observance of human rights. People who feel secure are more likely to enjoy greater happiness; and they will feel more secure if their rights are respected. But there are no absolute and inalienable human rights. 'All persons', wrote Mill, 'are deemed to have a right to equality of treatment except when some recognized social expediency requires the reverse.' On this view, 'Justice is the name for certain moral requirements which stand higher in the scale of social utility than others.'[16]

So much for those 'inalienable rights' of 'life, liberty and the pursuit of happiness' extolled in the American Declaration of Independence. Bentham described human rights as 'nonsense on stilts'; but it is those very human rights he so derided which are now considered to be the cornerstone of justice, and which are most likely to buttress whatever serious opposition there may be to the idea that the few may be abused for the benefit of the many.

THE LANGUAGE OF HUMAN RIGHTS

The notion of human rights has a curious history. There is no language of human rights until the fifteenth century, no words in Hebrew, Greek, Latin, Arabic or Old English which are equivalent to our modern understanding. The concept of human rights simply did not exist; nor inevitably did the language, in the centuries when the Bible was written, though it is possible to read back into the Bible the implication that people have rights. The book of Deuteronomy, for example, requires that a man's cloak, taken from him as a pledge, must be returned to him at night because he needs it to keep warm and without it he might die. The duty to give the cloak back may imply that he has a right to it.

The duties and responsibilities of society, and of individuals within society, feature largely in the Bible. It is eloquent about the resources, the possibilities, and the potential given in the created order, and about the sharing of those resources in acts of righteous love. Some great civil rights movements have been inspired by the Christian belief that every human being is created in the image of God, and is equally loved and embraced by God in the saving work of the Gospel.

It was the connections between Christian belief, human equality and human rights which gave such impetus to the work of Martin Luther King. It is the same link which gives power to the struggle for liberation in Latin America, in

Palestine and elsewhere now. But though the Bible is clear about righteousness, it remains silent about human rights, possibly for the same reason that Ghandi was not especially interested in rights. 'The true source of rights is duty,' he wrote. 'If we discharge all our duties, rights will not be far to seek. If leaving duties unperformed we run after rights, they will escape us like a will-o'-the-wisp. The more we pursue them, the higher they will fly.'[17]

Significantly, it was the Age of Enlightenment which spawned the classic language of human rights. Traditional understandings of authority were dissolving, which meant in turn that individuals enjoyed greater autonomy, greater control over their own lives, while scientific advances began to promise the means whereby that control could be made more effective. As the possibilities of such control increase, so the claims to human rights proliferate.

The most obvious example is the right to have children. Would people have talked in such terms fifty years ago? Today, techniques for assisting human reproduction become ever more sophisticated and more successful. What was largely a matter of nature in earlier years becomes nature assisted and to some extent controlled by technology. What used to be the gift of a child is now the right to have a child. As control increases, so expectations rise. Wants become needs; needs become rights.

The philospher Alasdair MacIntyre states bluntly that human rights are fiction. They do not exist, for precisely the same reason that unicorns and witches do not exist: 'that every attempt to give good reasons for believing that there are such rights has failed'.[18] Yet fundamental human rights – life, liberty and the pursuit of happiness – may be more than wishful thinking. Whether or not their existence can be established by reasoned argument, their roots lie in the simple fact of human existence. We have already explored the rational and theological arguments for holding that all human beings are equal. They are equal in their need for the most basic physical essentials which sustain life. They are equal too as moral persons. Human rights derived from a most basic understanding of human equality suggest that there is a right to life and a right to some freedom of choice. Otherwise, being human means very little.

IDEALS AND RIGHTS

John Habgood rejects the notion that these basic human needs can be turned into human rights.[19] He suggests that it is not human needs but human hopes and aspirations which form the most adequate basis for universal human rights. He points to the great potential in human nature, and to the capacity for human choice. Human life, he suggests, is an adventure in the realization of possibilities, and 'assertions of human rights are big steps in this adventure. They are instructions on the road to developing a more human and humane world'. They point to what might be.

It is helpful to elevate human rights by linking them to a vision of what might be, but ideals are a curious basis for rights. How can people have a right to pursue ideals which they may not even be able to define with any clarity, ideals which, as Habgood emphasizes, are 'open-ended'? His rejection of needs as defining rights, because there is, he says, no agreement even on what are basic human needs, does seem unnecessarily sophisticated. Very large numbers of people would gladly settle for life and some freedom of choice as their basic human rights.

Such fundamental human rights are, by definition,

universal. They apply to everyone, simply as human beings, and it is the claim to universality which gives the language of human rights its power. The Universal Declaration of Human Rights, originally agreed by the United Nations in 1948, is now the most widely accepted affirmation of the rights of people. But while the recognition and assertion of basic human rights may be a cornerstone of justice, and an important counterbalance to the prevalence of utilitarian theories, it does not solve all problems.

Rights are what must be achieved if there is to be any element of justice in society, particularly the right to life, liberty and equality before the law. Ideals tell what might be achieved in a society where there is perfect justice. Goals and objectives indicate what are considered to be realistic aims. But where does equality of opportunity fit into this pattern of ideals, objectives, and rights?

In an ideal society there would be equal opportunity for all to achieve their full potential. Equal rights in such a good society would mean that a black child and a white child, or a boy and a girl, would have equal opportunity in education. Since most societies are not ideal, realistic objectives would seek to extend and improve equality of opportunity in education. Or, to return to the chancellor's gaffe which sparked off this discussion about utilitarianism versus human rights, what about the complex question of equal opportunity in employment?

An ideal society would provide paid and good employment for everyone who wanted it. Realistic objectives require a recognition of the fact that there will never again be full employment in industrialized countries and that sharing the work which is available is the aim which might now be achieved. It is this side of justice, what Aristotle calls distributive justice, which is so complex and problematic, because it is concerned with the distribution of resources and goods and power, with employment and payment, with systems of government, with opportunities for personal fulfilment and happiness. Rights can more readily be applied to corrective justice, when liberty is unlawfully denied or people's lives are threatened. Beyond that basic level, the whole concept of human rights becomes more complex, not least because differing rights conflict with one another.

EQUAL AND DIFFERENT

It is here that we need to continue the exploration of equality which we began in chapter one, where we noted that in the natural world, equal does not mean the same. The Latin word *aequalis* does not mean 'same' but 'level', as in a level playing field. Equality would be virtually meaningless if everyone was the same. It is precisely the differences between people which make the concept of equality necessary.

Two golfers may be entirely different in physique, skill and experience. It is those very differences which must somehow be made equal if they are both to enjoy a game together. The handicapping system does precisely that. It encourages the differences by requiring the better player to allow strokes to the worse, giving them both an equal opportunity to win, and so requiring both to play to the best of their differing ability. But there are limits. Players whose game is not particularly good are given a maximum handicap of twenty-four. The same maximum is given to players who are simply dreadful. If the differences between two players are so great that really they fall outside the scope of the handicapping system, then the system is trying to tell them that there is little point in them even starting to play together.

The game of squash is so different from golf that a handicapping system is virtually impossible. If there is much difference between the two players, the better will coolly dominate the centre of the court, while the other hurtles around, vainly generating great heat, while losing one point after another.

In the natural world, there is no such thing as a handicapping system, or 'a level playing field'. The animal world is not governed by principles of equality or liberty. Nor is it always the fittest and strongest which survive. The survivors are those which make the most of unequal opportunities by adapting best to their environment. The nearest approximation to equal opportunities amongst animals occurs when one species is fortunate enough to find plenty of food. If there is not enough, then the strong will live and the weak will die.

Parallel situations have occurred amongst the human species in Western society in the past fifty years. In the 1950s, and again in the early 1980s concern about inequality declined, because there was plenty for everyone. Economic growth, more production and greater prosperity meant that almost everyone was better off. As J. K. Galbraith put it in *The Affluent Society*, 'increasing production has eliminated the more acute tensions associated with inequality'.[20] In a time of recession, those tensions recur, as the 1990s have so abundantly demonstrated.

'Inequality', said the German philosopher, Immanuel Kant, 'is a rich source of much that is evil, but also of everything that is good.'[21] The United Nations Declaration on Human Rights is so concerned to assign fundamental rights to everyone equally that it removes 'distinction of any kind, such as race, colour, sex, language, religion, political or other opinion, national or social origin, property, birth or other status'. The result is curious. The equal human beings who are entitled to rights are reduced to empty shells. They lack everything that makes for significance, for relationship; in short, humanity.

In the Dublin Zoo, there was once a keeper called Mr Flood, renowned for his skill in breeding lions in captivity. Asked the secret of his success, Mr Flood replied, 'Understanding lions.' Pressed to elaborate, he would say no more than 'Every lion is different.'

EQUAL OPPORTUNITY

It is the differences between people which makes the ideal of equal opportunities so difficult to sustain. If people are all of equal worth and dignity, they should all have equal opportunity to achieve their full potential. But since people are all different, equality of opportunity can only be achieved at the expense of personal liberty.

The ideal of equal opportunities is easily stated. But even if it were possible to create a society which did give everyone a genuinely equal opportunity, such a society would not continue in being for more than a few years, possibly not even that long, without sustained restrictions on personal liberty. People are different. Some would make great use of every opportunity. They would become wealthy, or powerful, or cultured, possibly even all three. Others would find their opportunities passing them by, unable or unwilling to take advantage of them. Some parents would encourage and stimulate their children, others ignore or stifle them. Family life is a source of great inequality in society.

To sustain a society which maintained genuine equality of opportunity would require the constant redistribution of wealth, power, and opportunity. It would involve removing from some people the opportunities they had gained, by legitimate means because of their ability, in order to recreate a level playing field for everyone. It would require a social system sufficiently strong and influential to level out the unequal influences of widely different family life; either that, or the abolition of the family altogether and the bringing up of children in some kind of communal life. Freedom to choose, and to enjoy or endure the consequences of that choice, would have to be severely restricted, and those restrictions would be imposed in the name of freedom for all.

John Rawls gets inside this problem by trying to create an imaginary situation in which people are equal in every respect, a Garden of Eden without the snakes. It is the great merit of his analysis that he begins by arguing, as we noted in chapter one, that all people are of equal value as moral persons. He does not set up an imaginary situation and draw from it the conclusion that human beings are equal. That would be, quite literally, a philosophical game. Instead, he begins with the conviction that all human beings are created equal, that 'each person possesses an inviolability founded on justice', and he argues persuasively for this conviction.

Then, because absolute equality cannot and does not exist in real life, he tries to imagine a situation in which people are genuinely equal; not the same, but equal. It is difficult even to imagine such a situation. Natural ability, family, culture, education and a great deal else all conspire to produce inequality from which no-one is ever entirely free.

TWO BASIC PRINCIPLES

Rawls himself suggests that if people were in a situation of genuine equality, or if they succeeded in imagining it, then they would agree on two basic principles. First, 'each person is to have an equal right to the most extensive total system of equal basic liberties, compatible with a similar liberty for all'.

All people want as much freedom as possible to develop their natural gifts, to exercise personal choice, to do whatever they choose to do, and to be themselves. The boundaries of that freedom are determined solely by the fact that everyone else will want the same measure of freedom.

The second principle is this: that 'social and economic inequalities are to be arranged so that they are of greatest benefit to the least advantaged, and attached to offices and positions open to all under conditions of fair equality of opportunity'.[22]

Clearly there are bound to be social and economic inequalities. People are different; and if, as the first principle maintains, they are to have as much freedom of choice as possible, then those inequalities will become progressively greater. If nothing is done to 'arrange' those inequalities, then before long some people will acquire the wealth and power which will give them great freedom of choice, while others will have very little.

Even so, this second principle is stated in a way which seems a little extreme, and Rawls himself, when he first sets it out, does put it rather differently: 'social and economic inequalities are to be arranged so that they are reasonably expected to be to everyone's advantage'. That is a much safer version. But in the course of his discussion it becomes clear that there has to be a bias in favour of the least advantaged, simply because the forces which result in ever-increasing inequality are so strong.

JUSTICE AS FAIRNESS

The thirty-two children, still squabbling over their forty bread rolls, could discuss for ever whether the great advantages of America and Europe, and the inequalities which result, are, in the long term, of benefit to everyone. At international conferences and in domestic politics, that reassuring argument is rehearsed at length. It is a most effective substitute for action. But if it were ever to be accepted that inequalities must be arranged so as to be of greatest benefit to the least advantaged, a world-shaking redistribution would have to take place.

Rawls claims to be setting out a concept of justice as fairness, and while they might not work through the five hundred or so pages of his book, children understand very well what fairness means. They put it into practice every time two of them have to divide a Mars Bar between them. One child has the knife, and decides where to cut the bar. The other child has first choice about which piece to take. For one child to have the knife and the first choice, simply because the other child is black, or female, or physically weaker, or not very bright, would be both unfair and unjust. It does not really need an Aristotle to point out that 'the person who acts unjustly gets too much, and the victim of injustice too little of what is good'.

The tendency towards inequality is so strong that even if people start out equal, before long one group will hold the knife, decide where to cut, and then have first choice as well. This is the comfortable position currently enjoyed by Western society. Rawls reworded his second principle precisely in order to provide a counterbalance to these forces of inequality.

Underlying both principles is the strong belief that in a society which values everyone as being of equal worth and dignity, freedom, opportunity, income and wealth should be shared equally. Inequality is only justified if it is to everyone's advantage. Injustice is inequality which benefits one individual or group rather than the whole of society.

Even with this explanation, the two principles remain open to question. It was said of Lord Rutherford, the famous scientist, 'Lucky old Rutherford! Always on the crest of a wave.' To which Rutherford replied, 'Well, I made the wave didn't I?' It is argued that the people who make use of their natural gifts are those who work hardest, who make their own waves, and who therefore deserve the wealth and power they acquire. Certainly such people should make a substantial contribution to society, but to arrange inequalities for the benefit of the least advantaged would be unjust. Hard work would not receive its just rewards. In the end, everyone would be harmed, because people with great natural ability might be reluctant to use their gifts to the full.

Moreover, suppose it is laziness or stupidity which results in some being disadvantaged. Why should the State compensate the indolent? If society is to be organized so as to allow maximum freedom and choice for everyone, why should the State interfere in the consequences of that choice, whether those consequences be wealth or poverty, a penthouse in Knightsbridge or a cardboard box in Waterloo?

AN EQUAL RIGHT TO JUST DESERTS

This is, of course, precisely the argument set out by Robert Nozick, whose views have been set against those of Rawls. Nozick maintains that in a just society, every individual has an equal right to keep and use whatever he or she has legitimately acquired. The only question is whether wealth, property or power were gained legitimately in the first place.

It is, of course, a fact that large parts of the United States were acquired from American Indians by means whose legitimacy is dubious, to say the least; that many of the most destructive disputes, in Ireland, in the former Yugoslavia, in Iraq and Kuwait, in Israel and Palestine, are rooted in questions about the ownership of land; and that large tracts of farmland in Britain were removed from common ownership by a force which was scarcely legitimate. But whether or not there are legitimate entitlements does not invalidate Nozick's basic position: which is that everyone has an inalienable right to enjoy the fruits of his or her own labour, to choose how to use wealth or power which has been legitimately acquired, and to pass on to others whatever may be left.[23]

Throughout the 1980s British government policy was determined in large measure by three considerations: freedom, just entitlement, and the need for continuous growth. State control and State ownership were reduced or removed altogether in order to create the greatest practicable degree of competition and market freedom. 'You can't buck the market' became the rallying cry of the faint-hearted; and though market forces have a bad name for a variety of reasons, there is a coherent political philosophy at work, based on an attempt to combine aspects of justice with what will work best and be most useful.

The justice lies in just entitlement and freedom of choice. Without low inflation and sound money, just entitlement dribbles away. Money loses its value. Low inflation is achieved through real jobs, providing goods and services which people need and choose to buy at realistic prices. Seen in this way, market forces are the collective consequence of the free choice exercised by individuals.

Utility is served because if people are free to make choices, and free to keep the results of their work, they will work harder, society will become more efficient, the economy will grow, and there will be more for everyone. There may be more people unemployed; but there will be money for unemployment benefit, and resources for health care, education and other benefits.

Since this political philosophy is advanced on grounds of justice and utility, it may be held to account on both grounds. In 1979 there was rampant inflation, which was harmful to everyone. In the ten years that followed, inflation was reduced and sound money restored, taxes were cut (particularly those affecting the rich), living standards rose by thirty-six per cent, and public spending on education, health, and social welfare increased significantly in real terms. In theory, the significant increase in the wealth of society was supposed to 'trickle down', and so benefit everyone. What in fact happened in Britain and in America, where similar processes were at work, was that the rich grew richer and the poor poorer. Some wealth trickled down in increased public spending, but the larger part of the substantial increase in wealth was shared by the richest third of the population.

Figures from the British Department of Social Security show that between 1979 and 1991, living standards for the richest ten per cent of the population rose by sixty-two per cent in real terms. The poorest ten per cent suffered a loss in real income of fourteen per cent. Peter Townsend, Professor of Social Policy at Bristol University and author of *Poverty in the United Kingdom*, said: 'These figures give the final lie to claims about the trickle down effect. Whether the income of the poorest is measured before or after housing costs, they are worse off in real terms. The top ten per cent have made gains ten times greater than the second poorest ten per cent. The figures are astonishing. At no time in the past hundred years since income statistics were first collected has there been such a dramatic widening of the gap.'[24]

FEEDING THE SPARROWS

The 'trickle down' theory has been brutally caricatured by Professor Galbraith as 'broadly the doctrine that if the horses are fed amply with oats, some will pass through to the road for the sparrows'.[25] Professor Galbraith may be better at economics than ornithology, since sparrows cannot even digest oats. But that aside, his cartooning of the trickle down theory shows vividly that the poor are left with the droppings of society. It is a twentieth-century version of Dives and Lazarus, the poor eating the crumbs that fall from the rich man's table. In the contest symbolized by Rawls and Nozick, between justice based on need and justice based on entitlement, Rawls in the red corner,

Nozick in the blue, the blue corner won by an early knockout. Political life was and is largely controlled by the concept of personal freedom and just deserts.

The right to own property was one of the pillars of Conservative policy, and the electoral success of the Conservatives was due in large part to the people who had worked hard to buy their own homes. It was the new experience of owning a house which led significant numbers of marginal voters to switch from a traditional allegiance to Labour, thus ensuring electoral victory for the Conservatives throughout the 1980s. Home ownership was achieved by selling council houses and thus reducing the stock of housing which remained in public ownership; which explains in part the great increase in homelessness.

For most people, the ownership of property was one tangible sign of just deserts, and of the fact that hard work, enterprise, intelligence and effort were receiving their just rewards. It is a view which is entirely consistent with the simplest, oldest definition of justice; that justice consists in giving to every person what he or she deserves.

It was not only in domestic politics that just deserts ruled. The divisions between rich and poor nations were subject to the same criteria. Western countries, so the argument ran, can point to centuries of civilization, culture and scientific advance. Poorer countries remain poor because of their impoverished history, their corruption, their bad one-party government, and their civil wars. Certainly the rich or developed nations should provide aid, both financial and technological; but not at the expense of Western prosperity. Such prosperity is earned and deserved, and is in any case ultimately in the interests of poorer nations, because it will eventually trickle down for their benefit. The fact that this is an inadequate account of either Western history or

African civilization is of little account in this scenario. Myths are always more powerful than facts, particularly the myths people want to believe; and if the myths are supported by an appeal to justice, so much the better.

Critics of government policy pointed to growing inequality, homelessness and unemployment, and declared it unjust. They maintained that the unemployed and the homeless were not guilty of idleness, but were the victims of social policy. Such criticisms were scarcely heard, and when they were heard, were greatly resented. The concept of just deserts held sway. The comfortable and the influential majority believed in it.

Appeals in the name of a different understanding of justice, for fairer distribution of work and payment, for the remission of Third World debt, for technology appropriate to differing cultures, all met with limited success, for the simple reason that there is no clear moral consensus about justice. The situation now is little different from that which Karl Marx noted in the 1860s, when he told the English trade unionists that it is no use arguing on the basis of justice, because there is no agreement about justice.

DRAWING A CONSENSUS TOGETHER

There is however a clear consensus about justice which runs through the Biblical teaching, through the larger part of the tradition of the Church, and through the views expressed by philosophers such as John Rawls, a consensus which we have explored in this and the previous chapters, and which may be summarized as follows.

> Justice requires that the whole human community works together to create a society in which every individual has

the freedom, the opportunity and the resources to flourish as a human being. Justice requires that every individual should have the greatest possible personal freedom which is consistent with a similar freedom being available to everyone.

Freedom is to be exercised within the human community, and for the community; because every individual in the human community, without exception, is created in the image and likeness of God, is equally loved by God, and is therefore equal in worth and dignity at the most fundamental level. Freedom is also to be exercised within the whole created order, of which human beings are an integral and interdependent part.

In a free and just society of equal people, whose gifts and abilities differ, opportunities and rewards will not necessarily be shared equally; but serious inequalities in opportunity or wealth or power will not be possible, because such inequality is at the expense of the freedom of others, and is destructive both of the human spirit and of the life of the community.

A just society will have a special care for the weak and vulnerable, and will exercise that care not by encouraging private acts of charity, but by ensuring that such people are treated justly by the structures of society, and are valued as human beings within the life of the community.

A SHARP CONTRAST

Such a tradition of justice is sharply at odds with the mainsprings of government policy in the 1980s, with its emphasis on personal freedom, just entitlement and the need for continuous growth. For personal freedom is understood to be the freedom to succeed, the freedom of atomized individuals with differing natural gifts and abilities who are encouraged to use their abilities competitively, so creating a society of winners and losers.

Society is considered to be little more than a collection of individuals, and the principle of just entitlement is intended to encourage individuals to create wealth, which may trickle down and so benefit the whole community. But because it is divorced from any clear understanding of society and social justice, the strong incentive towards competition and acquisition only succeeds in making the poor much poorer and the rich a great deal richer.

It is in the emphasis on continuous economic growth that the contrast between modern society and the older traditions of justice is most marked, a contrast which takes us back to the children squabbling over the bread rolls, and to Aristotle's understanding of fair distribution. When Aristotle argues that justice in distribution must be in accordance with merit in some sense, he is quite clear about what constitutes merit. It is not the capacity to produce goods and make offerings to the great god of continuous economic growth. Merit is that virtue which is excellence, which results in a character measured not by goods, but by the good, by beauty and truth and goodness.

It is not primarily greed, or the desire to have more than their share, which concerns Aristotle, but the fact that people live and work so as to have more for its own sake. They are, he says, people 'eager for life but not for the good life. Desire for life being unlimited, they desire also an unlimited amount of what enables it to go on.'[26] He has no objection to the principle of just entitlement, far from it, only with the vice which makes people want more and more. The Greek word which he uses to describe this vice, the word *pleonexia*, means literally, having and wanting more. It is a precise description of a consumer society. It indicates the great gulf between the older tradition of excellence as the highest good, and the values on which a materialistic society has come to depend.

A JUST CLAIM TO THE HOLY LAND

These complex issues of justice, equality, and the sharing of opportunity and resources are focused more sharply in Israel/Palestine than anywhere else on earth, and it is the tense situation in that land which provides a summary of the issues we have been considering in this chapter.

Hebron today is a large town ugly with hatred and fear. The ancient Tomb of the Patriarchs in the centre of Hebron is part mosque, part synagogue, part church, though today it is only Jews and Moslems who fight over this holy site. All but a tiny number of Christians have fled. High above the massive stone building, yet another of Herod the Great's constructions, there is an Israeli armed guard, and more inside; though in February 1994, they failed to prevent the massacre, by a fanatical settler of twenty-nine Moslems engaged in their early morning prayers.

In 1929 sixty-nine Jews were massacred in their homes by Arabs. Jewish cemeteries in the town were desecrated, and the Avraham Avin Synagogue was used as a latrine. In the Six Day War of 1967 the town was captured by Israeli forces, and has been under occupation ever since. Jewish settlers have moved in, most of them into a large settlement on the outskirts of the town which has reclaimed the old Biblical name for Hebron, Kiriath-arba; though some settlers have moved into the heart of the old town to reclaim it in the name of Greater Israel. Not surprisingly, the town is now a centre for the most extreme Arab resistance movements.

Jews and Arabs do not regard each other as equals. Both claim just entitlement to the land with a passionate and unyielding determination. When the right of the Israelis to settle in Hebron was challenged at the United Nations, the Israeli ambassador waved a copy of the book of Genesis above his head in the assembly. The Jewish title deeds to the land are written in this book, he claimed, and he quoted the account of Abraham purchasing the cave of Machpelah 'from the people of the land' for four hundred shekels of silver.[27]

It is 'from the people of the land' that the Palestinians trace their descent. The Christian priest, Elias Chacour, was once asked by an aggressive Israeli policeman at Ben Gurion Airport how many generations of his family had lived in Palestine. The policeman spoke with mock courtesy and patience. 'Let me tell you a story,' Chacour replied. 'One of my forefathers was sitting outside his house one day. He saw a poor stranger tired, hungry and thirsty. My forefather called. The stranger came. He was given food and water, and a place to rest. And then my ancestor asked him his name. The stranger said his name was Abraham. He was coming from Mesopotamia, a Gentile among Gentiles.'[28]

Just entitlement to the land, by Jews and Palestinians, stretches back through thousands of years; but insistence on just entitlement alone will never create justice and peace, only more tension, hatred and death. Since 1948, and continuing to the present day, Jewish settlers have driven Palestinians from their lands by brute force. Sometimes they have purchased, legally. More often they have stolen land, confiscated it, settled it illegally. Settlements in Gaza, in

Hebron and all over the Occupied Territories are a provocative offence to the Palestinians. But Arabs too have done their utmost to drive Israel into the sea. From before 1945, when the Arab leader in Jerusalem called on all Arabs to help the Nazis and serve God by killing all the Jews, until they were defeated in the Yom Kippur War of 1973, the Arab countries which surround Israel have done everything in their power to destroy the Jews and so prolong their tragic story.

LIBERTY TO THE CAPTIVES

Jews and Palestinians share something else, apart from an entitlement to the land. Both long for liberation. For many Jews, the return to the Promised Land and the founding of the State of Israel are the new Exodus, a liberation from the oppression which they have always suffered as strangers in foreign lands. Palestinians too long for liberation from the oppression of Jewish occupation, from being treated as second class citizens in their own land which has suddenly been made foreign. They long for the recovery of their land, their dignity, their freedom. Many leading members of the Palestine Liberation Organization are Christians who see their work for liberation in terms of the Exodus.

Jews and Palestinians both claim the same land. Both have a just entitlement. Both use the same vocabulary of liberation, and many draw inspiration from aspects of the same theology. In an attempt to break this deadlock, both Jews and Christians have worked at a new understanding both of justice and of theology.

It was Christians in South America who first developed a Theology of Liberation. The name is derived from the proclamation of liberty to the captives, in Luke 4, and from the experience of the people of Israel as recorded in the book of the Exodus. Much of liberation theology sets familiar Biblical teaching in a new light, a light which comes from two main sources.

First, it recognizes the powerful reality not just of individual sin but of structural evil. The Catholic bishops who met at Medellín in 1968 talked about 'structures of sin' and 'institutionalized violence'. They not only resolved to resist such violence, but also recognized that the Church, as a powerful institution, is part of it, through complicity with the structures of power. In Puebla, in 1979, their determination to stand with the Christ who is present in the poor and the oppressed was given a name, The Preferential Option for the Poor, which is now a key phrase both within and beyond the Roman Catholic Church.

The phrase 'Bias to the Poor' is crisper, and it is used more frequently in the Anglican Church because Bishop David Sheppard took it as the title for one of his books; but its use has been associated with suggestions that it is God who is biased in favour of the poor. It has never been satisfactorily explained how this supposed divine bias may be reconciled with the belief that God loves and cares for all people equally, or the fact that Christ was equally concerned, in different ways, for the salvation of both rich and poor. It would be more accurate to say that God commands those who are well-placed in this world to express their love for their neighbours and for God by having a special concern, a preferential option, for the poor.

NOT PEACE BUT A SWORD

Liberation theology tells us powerfully that this concern must be expressed not simply in acts of private charity, but in a fundamental Gospel challenge to the structures of society which cause oppression. 'I am not come to bring peace,' said Jesus, 'but a sword.' That saying is linked to a verse in the prophecy of Micah (7:6) which tells of the younger generation rising against their elders. In a society where respect for elders was a sign of stability and peace, such rebellion was greatly feared, and its occurrence was regarded as a sign of the breakdown of the structures of society. Jesus, in this saying, welcomes such breakdown as being part of his purpose. 'With this saying Jesus resolutely refuses to give his blessing to and legitimate the status quo of an unjust and unpeaceful world.'[29]

Theology and the Church quickly become part of that status quo, a situation to which liberation theology presents its sharpest challenge. For liberation theology recognizes that the justice and the charity which are given to the poor, whether the poor like it or not, is neither just nor charitable, nor liberating. Theology belongs to the poor as much as to anyone else. The poor are not stupid, nor are they incapable. Theology should not be done for them by the powerful and gift-wrapped in tidy parcels. The task of theology is to enable the poor to discover their own truth, and so to find strength and dignity, courage and liberation.

But what happens to the poor when they become rich, to the oppressed when they gain liberty, to the weak when they become strong? The tragedy of the Jewish people in Israel is that they have so quickly become oppressors, and though a great many individual people reject and deplore this, they and the Palestinians are locked into a deeply destructive cycle of institutionalized violence from which the peace process may eventually provide a way of escape.

The crucial question for every attempt at liberation is how to gain liberty without creating new oppression, without continuing and extending the cycle of violence. Naim A'teek is an Arab Christian whose village was stolen and destroyed by Jewish settlers. There is a dreadful irony in the fact that his father was a goldsmith, and when he was driven out by the Jews, he was able to pack such wealth as he had in a pocket – in precisely the same way that generations of Jewish goldsmiths have themselves fled from the pogroms.

'The challenge to Palestinian Christians,' he writes, 'and indeed to all Palestinians and to all people in this conflict in Israel/Palestine, is: do not destroy yourself with hate; maintain your inner freedom; insist on justice, work for it, and it shall be yours.'[30] But it is clear from his book on Palestinian liberation theology that the justice Naim A'teek seeks is not mere justice, but that justice which is righteous love, without which no-one is truly free.

FIVE

JUSTICE TRANSFIGURED

It was the police helicopter which woke up George Holland, a plumbing company manager, well after midnight. He looked out, saw the police cars, and went on to his balcony to try out the video camera he had just bought. Never before has an amateur gained such an audience for his first home video. It lasted just eighty-one seconds and was screened worldwide. The blurred, grainy images showed four police officers battering a man as he lay on the ground. It was a routine occurrence in Los Angeles. The video made it into an international concern.

One year later, the police officers were tried on charges which could have resulted in up to seven years imprisonment. All four were acquitted. Immediately the verdicts were announced, parts of Los Angeles exploded. Four days of rioting, the worst in America this century, left fifty-three people dead, nearly two thousand people injured, and four thousand buildings gutted by fire. Large parts of the city looked like scenes from World War Two after the blitz. Dazed and shocked people stared at television pictures of the charred and smoking remains, and wondered what had happened to the American dream. Rodney King, the man whose beating was seen by millions, made an emotional appeal on TV at the height of the riots: 'Can we all get along?' His words were plastered across billboards for weeks.

Many of the questions of justice which we have considered, and some we have yet to explore, are contained within that one explosive incident and its destructive aftermath. In Los Angeles, black people are the largest element in an underclass which burgeoned in the 1980s, as the rich grew richer and the poor poorer. Some of the most conspicuous displays of affluence to be found anywhere in the world exist in a city which also has slum ghettos as bad as any in South Africa. Rodney King is black, the four police officers are white. Many of the police officers evidently consider black people to be both poor and worthless. The recorded comments of men out on patrol that night were typical. They talked about 'hunting niggers' and 'roasting Africans'. For all the great progress in race relations in America, the violence of King's arrest symbolized the continuing failure of both black and white people to look each other in the eye and recognize and accept each other's worth.

The officer who first stopped King that night happened to be a woman. Rodney King is a tall, big man, six foot three inches and twenty stone, and he was fooling about. Nonetheless this one policewoman had the situation well under control until seventeen other officers converged on the scene. Four of them, all men, abruptly swept their woman colleague aside and violence replaced the relatively calm and controlled use of necessary force.

Rodney King, as is now well known, was no saint. He was on parole from prison after being convicted of armed robbery. He was very drunk. Since that fateful night, he has been stopped several times for drunken driving and has been found guilty of other offences. The attempt to make him an icon of innocent black suffering has failed. The burden was more than he could bear. But justice which is made conditional on character, or wealth, or colour of skin, or physical size, is not justice. Rodney King was entitled to fair treatment, whatever his background.

TWO TRIALS

The division between rich and poor, racial conflict, the

relation between men and women, and equality before the law, are all questions of justice to which we have given some consideration. The arrest of Rodney King, and the two subsequent trials, also illumine the interaction between the life of a community and its capacity to do justice, which we have mentioned briefly in the case of the Birmingham Six and which now needs further exploration.

The first trial of the four officers was moved out of the city because the defence argued, with some justification, that their clients were unlikely to receive a fair trial in Los Angeles. The town to which the trial was moved was Simi Valley, twenty-five miles away, predominantly white, deeply committed to law and order. It is a place to which many firemen and police officers retire, and has been named as one of the two safest towns of its size in the whole of America. Ventura County, which includes Simi Valley, is 79.1% white and 2.3% black. The district of Los Angeles where King lives is 7.7% white and 68.7% black. Out of four hundred possible jurors, under ten were black, and none was selected.

Two different worlds met in the trial, two estranged communities. The result was that the trial proceeded at two levels, with two views of justice. At one level was the evidence; the video, the conflicting testimony of the participants and the witnesses, the legal arguments. At a deeper, more personal level, there were the fears and the prejudices of the members of the jury, and the mood of the community from which they came.

The lawyers who defended the police officers exploited this situation brilliantly. They blunted the impact of the evidence by showing the video to the jury again and again, the whole of it thirty times and parts of it over seventy times. At a deeper level, the defence was continually asking the jury, in all kinds of ways, one simple question: 'If this big, black thug had appeared in your town, what would you have wanted the police to do?' At that level, there could be only one answer. The jury acquitted the officers. Los Angeles and black America erupted.

The federal government, catching the new mood, proceeded to add a deeper level of injustice. On the slender pretext of pressing different charges, the federal government ordered a new trial; which meant, as the American Civil Liberties Union pointed out, that the officers were to be tried twice for the same offence. The new trial was returned to Los Angeles County, where young black people had donned T-shirts bearing the slogan, 'No justice, no peace'. The jury, ten white and two black, had no chance. They could hardly acquit again, and risk further riots. The mood second time round was determined not by the small-town fears of comfortable white America, but by the echoing experience of millions of black Americans who feared, like their ancestors before them, that they too could have been at the mercy of the violence of white men.

The mood of a community is a precarious, fragile basis on which to do justice. Pontius Pilate knew that. 'Who do you want me to release for you?' he asked the crowd, 'Barabbas, or Jesus who is called Christ?' They said 'Barabbas.' Pilate said to them, 'What shall I do with Jesus who is called Christ?' They all said, 'Let him be crucified.' He said, 'Why, what evil has he done?'; but they shouted all the more, 'Let him be crucified.' Pilate quickly realized that he was getting nowhere, and that 'a riot was beginning'; so he bowed to the mood of the crowd.[1]

TEACHING THROUGH PUNISHMENT

Crowds, groups, even committees (perhaps especially committees), will sometimes do things of which the individuals who make up those groupings would be deeply ashamed. There is abundant evidence to support this fact, from the Holocaust to the arrest of Rodney King; but a theoretical base was provided in a famous and controversial experiment conducted by Milgram in the 1960s. Like a great many people, he was puzzled by the fact that so many German people colluded with Hitler, and so made the Holocaust possible. He therefore devised an experiment to test the theory that German people are more compliant than others.[2]

The experiment involved a learner, a teacher and the experimenter. Both the learner and the experimenter knew exactly what they were doing. The teacher did not. Eventually over a thousand people, from all kinds of backgrounds, were tested one by one in the role of teacher. The routine was the same every time. Each one was told that he or she was taking part in an experiment to assess the connection between learning and punishment. They saw the learner being strapped into a chair and having cathodes attached to his body. The teacher was given an electric shock of 45 volts through one of the cathodes to prove that everything worked, and then went into another room with the experimenter. The teacher could no longer see the learner, and did not know of course that the electric current had been switched off.

The teacher was instructed to ask a series of questions to which the learner would respond by means of flashing lights. Every time the learner gave an incorrect answer, the teacher was to give an electric shock, and increase it by fifteen volts for every wrong answer. The switches were all clearly labelled from 15 to 60 – slight shock; and so on, up to 315 to 360 – intense shock; 375 to 420 – danger, severe shock; 435 to 450 – XXXX.

Before starting the experiment, Milgram asked 40 psychiatrists to predict what would happen. They said that no more than one person in a hundred would administer the highest level of shock.

The astounding result was that sixty-five people out of every hundred went on administering shocks up to the maximum. Some were deeply distressed about what they were doing, but they still went on. The learner, of course, sat comfortably in his room feeling nothing; but his acted 'reactions' were recorded so that they would always be identical, and they were played back to the teacher: an agonized scream at 285 volts, kicking and begging to be released at 300 volts, ominous silence at 315 volts.

The teacher was instructed to treat no response as a wrong response, and on they went, on and on, sixty five in every hundred giving shocks powerful enough to kill. Milgram began the experiment with Americans, intending to move it to Germany. He never did. The results with Americans made it unnecessary. But other researchers did repeat it in Germany where eighty five of every hundred teachers went to the highest levels. Researchers in Jordan, Italy and Australia found levels similar to those in America.

SUBMISSION TO LEGAL AUTHORITY

The study is shocking evidence of the power of social and institutional forces to make ordinary people behave in extraordinary ways. The experiment was conducted initially at Yale University, a place of considerable institutional power; and many of those who took part said afterwards that because it was at Yale, they thought it must be all right – not an entirely wise assumption. Others were persuaded to continue because of the official nature of the experiment, or the power of the experimenter.

Various modifications to the experiment produced lower rates of compliance with the experimenter's instructions. Moving it from Yale University lowered the rate from sixty-five to fifty. Bringing the learner into the same room as the teacher lowered it even more; though even then thirty people in every hundred went up to 450 volts. When the experimenter went out of the room, and the teacher was left alone to follow the instructions, few did so. But when the teacher was paired with an assistant who administered the shocks, so that the teacher was not actually doing the damage, ninety-five out of a hundred teachers went on to 450 volts.

Milgram himself drew one simple conclusion: 'A substantial proportion of people do what they are told to do, irrespective of the content of the act and without limitations of conscience, so long as they perceive that the command comes from a legitimate authority.'[3] That legitimate authority may be the pressure of a group or culture, or the decision of a committee. It may be some form of religious or political or domestic or family authority. It may simply be the pressure of the way things are.

Striking confirmation of Milgram's experiment was provided by investigation into the records of the Nazi Party. In 1928, 63 per cent of Nazi Party members were opposed to any harm being done to the Jews. 32 per cent were apathetic. 5 per cent were in favour of doing harm to the Jews. In 1942, the number of people opposed to hurting the

Jews had dropped to 26 per cent. The number apathetic had risen to 69 per cent. Those in favour of doing harm to the Jews remained constant at 5 per cent.[4] As Martin Luther King once said, 'We shall have to repent in this generation, not so much for the evil deeds of the wicked people, but for the appalling silence of the good people.' A small majority in Nazi Germany claimed legitimate authority, and the majority acquiesced apathetically.

Rodney King and the four policemen; Pontius Pilate; the experimenter and his teachers, both those who killed the learner and those who refused, were all individual people who were shaped, for good or ill, by different communities. Their behaviour at particular moments was governed by the forces which had shaped their lives, their character and their personality. The ultimate weapon in the armoury of Milgram's experiment, when the teacher became desperately anxious to stop, was to say firmly, in a matter-of-fact way, 'You have no choice.'

Do individuals or communities have any real choice about the way things are? Are poverty, hunger and starvation to continue indefinitely? Will Third World debt always cripple poorer nations? Will we ever live as part of the natural order, rather than as users and abusers of nature? Do individuals and communities have any real choice?

THE CULTURE OF CONTENTMENT

Opposition to any radical change in the way things are is extremely powerful. It no longer comes from a ruling elite, an upper class of landed gentry against whom the masses struggle. It comes from what Professor Galbraith has called

'The Culture of Contentment'.[5] The majority of people in Western society, including the majority of churchpeople, are now an integral part of opposition to change, an integral part of the culture of contentment, and it has a negative and positive dynamic.

The negative is the pervading sense of powerlessness in the face of so much suffering and evil. The Samaritan who stopped on the Jerusalem to Jericho road to help a man who had been mugged has for generations exemplified the good person who is disturbed and willing to get involved when he sees a victim of injustice lying in the road. 'Go and do the same,' we are told. What could be simpler! To protest, 'But it's not that simple' sounds like evasion. Evasive it may be, but it is no longer that simple. Today's victims of injustice are waiting to meet us at every turn.

A would-be good Samaritan may be woken by an alarm clock 'Made in China'. It is most likely that it was assembled by political prisoners, whose forced labour was repaid only by the opportunity to continue living and working. Buying it has rewarded those who exploited such labour, and has contributed minutely to the maintenance of a political system whose oppressive power became suddenly visible in Tiananmen Square.

Breakfast coffee is provided courtesy of growers and pickers in the Third World who probably did not receive a fair price for their labour. Meanwhile radio or television provide vivid accounts of the latest shooting in Northern Ireland, of riots in Los Angeles, of a missing child whose parents are asked how they feel, of famine in another African country, images and information half heard, yet seeping into the unconscious and deadening sensibilities. All that and more before the good Samaritan drives to work, using more nonrenewable resources and offering a tiny contribution to global pollution.

Before nine in the morning, the best intentioned person passes by countless victims of injustice, people beaten up by political systems, multinational corporations and market forces. Stopping to pull someone out of the ditch would make little difference to the systems which put them there. Passing by on the other side is no evasion. It just happens again and again. It is essential to survival. The alternative is to be consumed by guilt, powerlessness and futility. But the effect is deadening. Today's Samaritan is a victim too, senses battered, feelings blunted by so much suffering and so little power to do anything about it. This is the negative dynamic.

The positive lies in the fact that far from binding up wounds, even the best intentioned and most alert person is a beneficiary of the system and part of the culture of contentment. Professor Galbraith identifies the main characteristics of this culture as just deserts, limited vision, self-interest, and tolerance of inequality.

Just deserts is the belief, already noted, that hard work, enterprise and initiative deserve to be rewarded. Limited vision is another way of describing short-term policy, the view that expensive action and demanding changes in lifestyle may be important and necessary for the long-term future, but they are of less importance than comfort now. Dire predictions about the year 2010 may not come true.

Self-regard is related particularly to the role of the state. Removing state control and reducing the responsibility of government has been a major political activity during the past ten years in Britain and America, particularly in reaction against the nanny state, partly because of the belief that the state should not do what individuals, groups and organizations can do for themselves. Limiting state provision and encouraging private enterprise is generally supported by the comfortable majority because it reduces taxation and because the comfortable majority has the knowledge and the resources to make this system work to its own advantage.

Tolerance of great inequality in wealth is a necessary part of this package. It is a remarkable fact that there is so little outcry about the huge salaries and bonuses paid to some senior executives, and so little protest about the rapid widening of the gulf between rich and poor. Even muted protest is quickly silenced by comments about the politics of envy. The reason which Professor Galbraith gives for this tolerance of inequality is that any argument in favour of imposing higher taxes on the rich also makes those who are comfortably off more vulnerable. 'The plush advantage of the very rich is the price the contended electoral majority pays for being able to retain what is less but what is still very good.'[6]

There are of course voices raised in protest at this culture of contented self-interest. Such voices are heard, and valued as giving credibility to the democratic process. But they make little real difference. The policies pursued are those which the comfortable majority wants, and can secure by voting power.

A political party which stated in its election manifesto that it would release Third World countries from the repayment of debt, and would encourage other countries and business corporations to do the same; that it would increase aid for development; that it would work for just dealing in international trade; and that it would pursue domestic policies which created greater social justice – such a party could be sure of one thing only, that it would have committed electoral suicide. The negative and positive dynamics which oppose radical change are powerful. They are part of the Western way of life. This is the way things are. But does it have to stay this way? Is Milgram's experimenter right when he says, in a matter-of-fact way, 'You have no choice'? Do we have to continue with political systems which are bankrupt, with lifestyles which are destructive of human life and of the environment?

If Milgram's compliance rates are any guide, it is likely to be the case that the people who work for a more just society will always be among a minority of insurgents, of nonconformists, of people who are willing to challenge legitimate authority and the way things are. A more just society will be the work not of the contented majority, but of a minority made uncomfortable either by the lack of this world's goods, or by political or religious convictions.

NEW COMMUNITIES

At the end of MacIntyre's book, *After Virtue*, there is a famous paragraph which has often been quoted. It follows his pessimistic conclusion that there is no moral consensus in our society, nor the resources to develop one; and that not only Marxism, but every other political tradition within our culture is exhausted. He then points out that as the darkness descended on the Roman Empire, a crucial turning point occurred when men and women of good will stopped supporting the status quo, and set themselves to construct 'new forms of community within which the moral life could be sustained. We too have reached that turning point. What matters at this stage is the construction of new forms of community within which civility and the intellectual and moral life can be sustained through the new

Dark Ages which are already upon us.'[7]

The most effective modification Milgram introduced into his experiment was to provide the teacher with two colleagues. Instead of an individual caught in social and institutional forces, there was a small community of three. After a while, both colleagues, acting on Milgram's instructions, refused to continue, and though the experimenter ordered the teacher to go on, nearly all stopped. 'I didn't know I could stop', said one, 'until the other two refused to go on.'

It was three people working together in the last century who first coined the phrase, Christian Socialism. Like many others in that earlier age in injustice, they were determined to work for change. Individually they were gifted, capable men. Together they were a force. One was F. D. Maurice, a professor, a shy man whose theology was profound, his sermons obscure. Another was John Ludlow, a radical socialist, practical, deeply committed. The third, later to become famous as an author, was Charles Kingsley, a passionate and romantic idealist full of energy and good intentions. 'Ludlow proffered the social ideas, Kingsley the prophetic fire, Maurice the anchorage in Christian doctrine. In this unusual crew, Ludlow stood at the helm, Kingsley flew the flags and sounded the horn, Maurice poked around in the engine room to see that the engines were of authentic Christian manufacture.'[8]

A substantial number of people joined these three, though they were eventually shipwrecked by the forces of conservatism and by the internal tensions of their own group. They never succeeded in forming a community strong enough to hold them together. But during their brief voyage they moved in the right direction, and their shipwreck serves as a warning.

A community is far more than a team of like-minded people working towards the same end. The experience of the first Christian Socialists and the teacher working with colleagues demonstrate the great importance of people working together, but such groupings do not match up to MacIntyre's call, repeated by a great many people, including religious leaders, for new forms of moral community to meet the demands of our age.

But why 'new'? The multiplication of groups, churches, sects and societies has already reached epidemic proportions. Do we need yet more? And for how long will they remain new? Perhaps new really means forms of community which can understand the new situation we have to face, and respond to it creatively. That new situation is fluid, changing and fragmented. Twenty years ago it was thought that religion and secular society were two self-contained systems moving further and further apart, becoming more polarized, with fewer and fewer points of contact. Suddenly the idea that there are separate worlds is unreal.

The supreme example of this is that the confrontation between monolithic systems, Capitalism and Marxism, Christianity and Communism, East and West, with its Cold War and its Iron Curtain, has dissolved; and as the two systems intermingle, both need rethinking. The idea that a secular society would be complete in itself, free from religious influence, is undermined by what Dr Jonathan Sacks has described in his Reith lectures as 'the persistence of faith'. The values of a secular society are still to some extent derived from and sustained by communities of faith; while those communities in turn are profoundly influenced for good and ill by the impact of secular society.

At one level, modern society is moving in the direction

of more collective enterprise, a mass-media culture, greater economic interdependence, less individual power. Walk through any major shopping area in Britain, and at least half the stores, all under various names, are owned by just two different holding companies. Common Markets, multinational companies and rapid social change all shape a society which compounds the injustices human beings have always inflicted upon one another, and which makes social justice far more complex than the sum total of individual acts.

Paradoxically, those same forces are creating a plural, diverse and fragmented society. Science and technology offer greater control over human destiny, but the price is unending instability. The circumstances of life change rapidly, making us harassed and restless. New forms of community, if they are to be useful and effective, must respond to this situation.

A WORLD WITHIN THE WORLD

The most remarkable growth in new forms of community during the past twenty years has been in sects, in New Age groups, in house churches, and in various forms of religious fundamentalism. What these diverse communities have in common is a rejection of the values of society, and the establishing of alternative beliefs, values and lifestyles. Such communities provide security, refuge and mutual care. Individuals who join one of these groupings frequently discover a sense of belonging and of personal identity, security and power.

These communities are like a world within a world. That is their strength and their appeal, but also their weakness.

They put themselves on the margins of society, and are not likely to work for change from within society. If they do work for social change, it will be by trying to impose their standards; but they are more likely to function like 'snatch squads', rescuing individuals from the evils of society or from what they consider to be the corruption of the churches. Such communities fail to address the reality of contemporary life. They react against it, divorcing themselves from it, and creating their own separate world with its own distinct values.

Forms of community which will serve the pursuit of justice for the future will have to work within society. They will be flexible, diverse, and they will need to make use of the best available insights, wherever they may be found. There will be no room for philosophical or scientific imperialism of the kind displayed by such scientists as Dr Richard Dawkins. His lively and entertaining refusal to allow that theologians might occasionally talk some sense, and his categorization of people who believe in a Creator God as 'know-nothings', 'know-alls' and 'no-contests' is a denial of the partnership between science and religion which is now at last possible.[9] Fortunately there are few scientists and probably no philosophers who would consider their own insights to be the only valid form of knowledge.

There will be no room either for that Christian imperialism which lays claim to a monopoly of truth. It is a fundamental Jewish and Christian belief that God is the Creator of all people, and that intelligence, creativity and a capacity for love and justice are gifts given by God to everyone. Truth therefore is neither limited to nor the possession of the community of faith. If it is suggested that people of faith have access through their beliefs to pure streams of truth which are denied to those without faith, then neither the evidence of history nor the experience of human society supports such a suggestion. 'For the past century', write Dr Sacks, 'religion has been embattled and defensive. This has led to the two religious stances most common in the modern world, a diffuse liberalism on the one hand, sanctifying secular trends after the events; and a reactive extremism on the other, willing us back into a golden age that neither was nor will be again.'[10]

A COMMUNITY OF WORSHIP

Is it possible then that the older religious communities, carrying such a great weight of accumulated tradition and culture, can serve the pursuit of justice into the next century? Is it conceivable that they will become the flexible, diverse, open communities which are needed? The greatest hope lies in the simple fact that what distinguishes religious communities from all other groupings and societies is the life of worship. Other communities, universities for example, medical colleges, trade unions, and ancient guilds, have a continuity of community life and of shared beliefs.

It is worship that is central to any religious community, worship which is closely connected with beliefs and values, worship which creates and sustains Christian communities. For worship expresses belief and belief gives substance and meaning to worship; while belief and worship together nourish the values which are expressed in the lifestyles, cultures and policies of the community. Dr Sacks ends his Reith lectures on an optimistic note: 'Religions are the structures of our common life. In their symbols and ceremonies, the lonely self finds communion with others who share a past and a future and a commitment to both. Faith persists, and in persisting allows us to build a world more human than one in which men, nations or economic systems have become gods.'[11]

If faith communities are to share in building a more human world and a more just society, they will need to focus clearly on those traditions and beliefs, ways of worship and patterns of community life which serve the cause of justice; which may mean attending more carefully to what is happening now, and building on it, rather than rushing into the assumption that something new must be done. The continuity of faith and the weight of tradition may be more relevant to justice than is sometimes recognized.

A business executive with substantial responsibility belonged to his village church and shared in its life and worship. He would generally be in church for the eucharist on Sunday morning. On Monday he might be in London, or America, or the Middle East, involved in international business deals of great importance and complexity. The decisions of the corporation which he chaired had far-reaching consequences and contributed significantly to either justice or injustice in one Middle Eastern country in particular.

After a week of travel and negotiation, he would be in church at the eucharist again. 'I don't want the Church to change,' he once said 'everything else in my world changes fast. I need the Church to stay the same'. There was nothing rigid about it. He would have had little patience with Christians who insist that everything must always stay exactly the same. He would have laughed at the church where the vicar, knowing that moving the lectern to a slightly more central position two feet away from the wall would be fiercely resisted, moved it a few centimetres each week and hoped no-one would notice.

Like a great many people, that businessman wanted a liturgy which was constant, celebrated with meaning and without fuss, a sermon which reminded him of the world of faith and made him think, and an opportunity to touch deeper reality. Tradition, belief and worship were the means whereby his values were both challenged and affirmed. He neither expected nor wanted the Church to say anything directly about the complex work in which he was engaged. Whether he was right about that is perhaps open to question; but his view of tradition and belief gives to both a significance easily ignored.

NOURISHING VALUES

The accumulated traditions of the Church, its structures and creeds, its liturgies, hymns and prayers, its culture and its building give continuity to the community and nourish the values which direct people's actions in the world. But that tradition can easily be used to escape into the past, to create a culture of ecclesiastical contentment and to serve particular interests.

To do this, it is necessary only to make a careful selection of parts of the tradition, and ignore the rest. A classic example was the Prime Minister's speech to the Church of Scotland General Assembly in 1988.[12] A careful interpretation of the Creation stories and of the death of Christ emphasized the freedom of individuals to make choices; the parable of the Talents was used to value individual enterprise and initiative; John Wesley was pressed into service to justify hard work, thrift and the creation of wealth; and Christian responsibility in society was reduced to 'most Christians would regard it as their personal

Christian duty to help their fellow men and women'. Though the phrase did not surface at any point in the speech, the conclusion to which the argument pointed was that 'there is no such thing as society'.

Such a conclusion rightly emphasizes the importance of individual responsibility; but it is contradicted by experience, such as the Los Angeles riots and the trials of the police officers; by the social sciences generally and experiments such as Milgram's in particular; and by the Jewish and the Christian traditions.

In the Hebrew and the Christian understanding, to do justice is, as we have seen, to live with God and with other people in relationships of righteous love. The book of Deuteronomy encourages individuals to relieve the needs of the poor but also sets out laws intended to create a more just society. God's choice and call is addressed initially to Abraham as an individual, but through him to a people, and through them to an entire world. God's offer of grace and love is addressed to individuals by name; but every individual who responds to that offer becomes part of a body of Christ through baptism into the Church.

At the central act of Christian worship, individuals receive the bread and the wine, and each individual is responsible to God and to other people for his or her own life. But the eucharist is celebrated by the community. Without a community, there can be no eucharist. The bread and the wine are received from other people and with other people, in community. The suggestion that there is no such thing as society is an aberration created by political ideology. It is also a view held by people who want to make their personal communion without having to engage with other people at anything more than a superficial level. Such individualistic views ignore the subtle and sustained interweaving of the life of society with individual responsibility, which is an integral part of Jewish and Christian belief.

PRIVATE CHARITY OR SOCIAL ACTION?

The consequences of separating individuals from society, and of overemphasizing individual freedom, have been serious and remain so. The seeds of such thinking were sown in the seventeenth and eighteenth centuries, not only by the new insights of the Enlightenment, but also by the failure of the Churches to come to terms with the rise of capitalism. Instead of thinking hard about the new social and economic order which was rapidly developing and expanding into Africa, India and the Americas, the Church merely continued to treat every transaction, no matter how large it might be, as a matter of personal conduct to be governed by the traditional rules of personal piety.

In such thinking, social justice becomes not the creation of a just society, but the sum total of those individual acts which are intended to remedy injustice. Individual piety becomes more significant than social responsibility, and social justice becomes an extension of individual piety. Justice is replaced by acts of private charity intended merely to remedy injustice. Even more serious, Christian faith may become so irrelevant to larger questions that it is confined to matters of personal morality; and when the Church begins to recover, and starts to make a contribution to wider debate, politicians will tell church leaders to keep out of politics.

It is of course much easier if the Church does keep out, not only for the politicians but also for the Churches. If a church arranges to care for the homeless, then people brought off the streets to a place where there is food or warmth may be grateful. But to challenge policies which create homelessness will arouse opposition. It is difficult, hard work, but still relatively easy to set up a shelter for the homeless; extremely difficult and very hard work to acquire the information and gain the support needed to challenge the systems which cause homelessness.

It is easier to operate from the position of power and control nearly always enjoyed by those who try to do good to others; but it is hard, and can be threatening personally, to challenge powerful structures. Churches generally are not good at managing conflict, much better at helping casualties.

Throughout the eighteenth century, the Church generally emphasized personal piety, avoided conflict, and colluded with injustice in the structures of society. Charity replaced justice. R. H. Tawney, in his classic study of *Religion and the Rise of Capitalism*, is scathing. 'In the eighteenth century', he writes, 'it is almost superfluous to examine the teachings of the Church of England as to social ethics. For it brings no distinctive contribution, and the very conception of the Church as an independent moral authority, whose standards may be in sharp antithesis to social conventions, has been abandoned.'[13] It is ironic that while the Church of England is still recovering those parts of its tradition and belief which set individuals and society in proper relationship, political ideology should be laying such unbalanced emphasis on individual enterprise, to the detriment of society.

A DREAM OF JUSTICE

If Tawney was scathing about the Churches, Laski was devastating, and his criticism touches a different area of Christian belief and its connection with social justice. Harold Laski was a somewhat waspish intellectual, who once wrote that 'no influence was more persuasive than that of Wesley in inducing the masses in England to accept the grim discipline of the new factories in exchange for the dubious consolations of an unproved and unprovable eternal bliss'.[14] It was an acid comment, though not entirely lacking in justification.

Much Christian teaching on matters of justice has been overshadowed by the futility and transience of this world when compared with the glories of the next. St Paul on marriage and slavery, St Augustine on the City of God, John Wesley on the glories of heaven, all represent a tradition which makes the eternal city far more significant than this world. Again, it is the emphasis on one aspect of Christian belief which is destructive. Belief in a life beyond death is an integral part of Christian faith for many reasons, not least because if God is a God of justice, there must be a future life in which the injustices of this world are remedied. But the conclusion is then drawn that because slaves will be free in heaven, because the lame will dance in the new Jerusalem and the poor will feast on good things, we need do little about injustice now.

Such views are no longer so influential as once they were, but that is partly because we no longer have so clear and inviting a mental picture of heaven. 'Where our fathers saw gleams of gold', wrote C. S. Lewis, 'we see only the mist, white, cold, featureless and never moving.'[15] Lewis connects the decline of a vivid belief in heaven to the loss of hope;

and though we have rightly abandoned using heaven as an excuse for condoning injustice now, we have also lost the incentive and the hope such belief provided. For the dream of perfect justice in the heavenly city is an inspiration and a promise, while the achieving of a measure of justice in this world gains greater sparkle for being a pledge and a sign of that perfect justice which will one day be glorious reality. To work for justice is to anticipate and to prepare for that perfect justice of which we see now only tantalizing but inspiring glimpses.

SUFFERING MARTYRS

There is one other aspect of Christian belief so central to the pursuit of justice, so ambiguous in its effects, that it requires particularly careful exploration. Christian redemption is offered not because of a triumphant struggle over injustice, not because of a long and successful campaign to change society, not because of political or diplomatic skill, but because of the suffering of one man. Like the belief in heaven, that suffering has been used to encourage endurance in the face of injustice.

Biblical texts such as 'take your share of suffering as a good soldier of Jesus Christ' (2 Timothy 2:3), or that mysterious comment about rejoicing in suffering which 'completes what is lacking in Christ's afflictions' (Colossians 1:24), have been used for centuries to justify passivity in the face in the face of injustice and oppression. A key element in Christian piety, particularly in the Middle Ages, has been quiet submission to the suffering caused by injustice: 'because Christ also suffered for you, leaving you an example, that you should follow in his steps' (1 Peter 2:21).

It is no longer so, though the extreme reaction against such piety may be just as unhealthy. Suffering is now unfashionable because it contradicts the prevailing desire and determination for happiness. Where earlier generations were encouraged to endure suffering with patience, today's sufferers are told to cheer up. The pursuit of happiness requires that suffering be suppressed, denied or hidden. But neither passive acceptance nor cheery denial is true to the meaning of the Cross.[16]

Passive submission to injustice is utterly different from the acceptance of the suffering which is caused by fighting against injustice. The piety which makes a virtue of passive submission is destructive, dehumanizing. Christ did not suffer passively. He cried out to be spared. He did not want to die. Christians in Latin America have suffered terribly in this century in the struggle for justice. Many have died. They did not want to die. On the table of Luis Espinal was an unfinished letter, found soon after he was murdered: 'The faithful do not have a vocation to be martyrs. Life ought to be given by working, not by dying. But if the day comes when they must give their lives, they will do it with the simplicity of someone who is carrying out one more task, without melodramatic gestures.'[17]

Christians in Latin America do not submit passively to injustice. They value themselves more highly than that. They know that they are loved and valued by God, that they have dignity and worth no less than those who oppress them. So they work for liberation, for the freedom to be the people they are. And they work for the liberation of those who cause injustice and grow rich from it, so that they too will be free to be truly human. In that struggle, they gain strength from the sufferings of Christ and from his acceptance of them. Because of the Cross they know that

Christ has suffered, and still suffers with them.

'A BEAUTIFUL GOSPEL TIME'

The suggestion, frequently made, that the sufferings of Jesus were unique, greater than all other suffering, is curious and sometimes macabre. A priest once tried to console a frail, elderly person by saying to her that Christ had suffered too. She was not consoled. 'Did he grow old slowly?' she asked. The sufferings of Christ, the loneliness, the loss of certainty, the physical pain, the spiritual desolation are not unique, nor worse than all other suffering. They are part of the common experience of all people.

As Christ hangs naked on a Cross, poor and utterly powerless, the poorest of the poor know that Christ is with them and for them. But even the poorest have more reason for hope than did the dying Christ. Father Joao Burnier was murdered when he went to a police station to protest at the mistreatment of two women. 'He died for justice and charity,' said his bishop. 'The Lord is the resurrection and the life. This is not a sad time but a beautiful gospel time.'[18]

Jesus, dying on the Cross, had no way of knowing that his death would be followed by 'a beautiful gospel time'. It is true that the gospels record his prediction, repeated three times, that he would be killed and would rise again on the third day. But even if he did say those words, if they were not written into the text by the gospel writers in the light of the Resurrection, they were still statements of faith by Jesus, and not of fact. He could not know for certain what might happen after his death. There were no precedents for the Resurrection, apart from the somewhat fishy experience of Jonah which the gospels connect with the three days in the tomb.

The last words from the Cross, which would also have been said on that same Friday evening by Jewish children as they went to sleep, were an act of faith: 'Father into your hands I commit my spirit.' The sufferings of Jesus are seen now in the light of the Resurrection. There was no such light when Jesus died, no certainty. But there was acceptance. And there was hope.

Christ's acceptance of suffering was positive, not passive. Jesus in Gethsemane prayed to God to spare him and asked his friends to support him. Both requests were denied. But his deep love for God, his oneness with God, carries him through despair and desolation into acceptance. Jesus on trial, Jesus on the Cross, is not a submissive, passive man. He is a man who has looked evil full in the face and has accepted the challenge. He has taken hold of the cup. He has decided to drink. It is a deliberate act of will, inspired by love.

Acceptance of this kind does not turn suffering into something good, the irrational into something rational and purposeful. The causes of suffering remain a great evil. But acceptance takes the power away from those who cause suffering. Pilate, used to exercising power, used to seeing men cower or submit, is puzzled. He did well to be puzzled. For the love which lies at the heart of Christian acceptance is more resilient than the denial of justice, more powerful than torture, stronger than death. Jesus has desired not to die. His desire is not met. He still loves; and his love, being stronger than any particular desire, is free.

A REVOLUTIONARY LOVE

The person whose love for God reaches this level is, paradoxically, more likely to work for change, not less. To love God without imposing conditions on the ways in which God will act is true freedom. It is this love which is revolutionary, in the literal sense of that word. It is free to dream dreams, to see visions, to hope for the absurd. It can shake earthly powers. It did just that in pagan Rome. It has done so again in recent times in Latin America.

In a pastoral exhortation in 1978, Cardinal Landazuri wrote: 'To carry the Cross is not simply to endure the inevitable hardships of life: it is also, and in present circumstances must be, to accept the sufferings imposed by the struggle against injustice and oppression'.[19] The acceptance exemplified in the love of Christ is beyond the reach of human power. Through that love, Christians are 'more than conquerors'. Like St Paul, Christians in Latin America are convinced that 'neither life, nor death, nor angels, nor principalities, nor things present, nor things to come, nor power, nor height, nor depth, nor anything else in all creation, will be able to separate us from the love of God in Christ Jesus our Lord' (Romans 8:38-9).

It is this depth of faith which refutes the criticism, frequently made, that people who work for justice are materialistic, concerned only with politics, Marxists thinly disguised as Christians. Such criticism has been levelled at Christians in South Africa, in Britain, as well as in Latin America. It is true that the poor in Latin America are materialistic. Without bread, housing and medicine, they die. It is true that Christians in South Africa are concerned with politics, for the oppression of black people is political. It is true that Christians who press for the redistribution of wealth can sometimes sound like Marxists. But such political materialism is an expression of faith, not a denial of it.

Behind such criticism lies a major question about the

relationship between the life of faith and the struggle for justice, between personal piety and social change, between the work of evangelism and working for a just society. In the past hundred and fifty years, every possible permutation of the connections between faith and working for justice has been tried, and argued for with passionate intensity.

JUSTICE AND EVANGELISM

A robust gentleman named R. N. Cust, a staunch supporter of missions in the 1890s, represents the view that the business of the Church is evangelism, pure and simple. In 1888, in his *Notes on Missionary Subjects*, he declared that the mission of the Church is to convert souls. 'I am entirely in favour of the lay evangelist, of the female evangelist, the medical evangelist, whenever gospel preaching is the substantive work; but when it is proposed to have a pious industrial superintendent, or a low church raiser of cattle or breeder of turnips, I draw my line.' It is a clear line. Over the door of every mission school he would have written, 'Those who enter here, sooner or later, must become Christians.'

It was education with a view to conversion, and injections of medicine and the Gospel, which gave rise to Ghandi's criticism: 'Why should I change my religion because a doctor who professes Christianity as his religion has cured me of some disease, or why should the doctor expect or suggest such a change while I am under his influence? Proselytizing under the guise of humanitarian work is unhealthy. It is most certainly resented.' To those on the receiving end, evangelism and social action seem to lean on each other like cripples. Both appear deformed.

It was partly in reaction against this that a view developed, now widely held, that to work for social justice is the most effective of evangelism. An enquiry published in 1932 under the title *Re-thinking Missions* stated that 'ministry to the secular needs of man in the spirit of Christ is evangelism in the right use of the word'. The proclamation of the Gospel is no longer essential. 'The Protestant missionary', wrote a critic, 'now tries to create an environment rather than to save souls. World evangelism requires a change of sanitation quite as much as a change of heart.'[20] Underlying this view is a coherent theology which holds that the ultimate aim of God's mission in the world is more than personal salvation; it is justice, peace and wholeness for all people and for all the created order. To work for justice is to work with God, and if the Church is part of that work, then the Gospel is proclaimed.

These different permutations are right and important in what they emphasize, wrong in what they deny or ignore. John Wesley preached for personal conversion and did so with great power. His ministry has been rightly criticized for ignoring larger questions of justice and for leaving decisions to the individual conscience. He was a child of his time, with little awareness of social structures or social justice. He had no intention of involving the Church in politics; yet out of the revival his preaching started, and through the renewal of personal faith, came the evangelical movement with its long political campaigns, first for the abolition of slavery, then for the reform of prisons.

FROM JUSTICE TO FAITH

Sometimes the move is in the opposite direction, a concern

for justice raising sharp questions about personal faith. The senior management team of a dynamic and successful business was greatly concerned about growing unemployment in the city where they were based. They invited a Christian priest to meet with them to discuss it. Forty people were present, almost the whole of the management team, few of whom were Christians. Many had friends in other companies who had been made redundant. They were concerned, not only for their friends, but also for their own jobs.

After some discussion, the Finance Director of the company suggested that if everyone in the room agreed not to accept the annual increase in salary which would soon be due, they could employ fifteen more people. There was a thoughtful silence. The Sales Director said he could use more sales staff, and with increased sales, the future of the company would be more secure. The priest commented that the choice was about what they really wanted, and therefore was, to some extent, about what kind of people they were. No-one raised any objection to what was suggested; and no-one did anything. Salary increases were paid as usual and their concern about unemployment faded.

It is possible, of course, that they might have decided to reduce their own salaries and increase employment without any of them becoming Christians, either out of a concern for justice, or to safeguard the future of their own employment, or a combination of the two. But they did nothing. They lacked the will or the motive or both. If more of them had been Christians, if more had loved God and their neighbours, they might have persuaded the rest to do something.

It would of course have been necessary for the whole company to act together. Had they done so, and reduced their own standard of living in order to benefit others, that would have been a major reversal of prevailing social philosophy (based largely on personal self-interest, not to say greed). It would have been a small step in the direction of reducing inequality between those in paid work and the unemployed. Although the decision was left to the individual conscience, the consequences would have made some modest changes to the structures of society. To that extent, it was different from John Wesley's famous sermon on the use of money – 'get all you can, save all you can, give all you can', where giving eases the consequences of injustice and charity is a substitute for creating a just society. It was a dour Scottish professor who once remarked that 'charity is wasting your substance on riotous living'.

Whether the beginning is a concern about injustice which then leads to personal faith, or whether the starting point is personal conversion and the end is social justice, Christian faith is emphatic that both belong together. Evangelism is often defined as the proclamation of the good news of the death and the Resurrection of Jesus Christ so that people will trust in Christ and serve him in the world in the fellowship of the Church. In this classic definition, to work for justice is a result of conversion.

It would be more helpful to see the work of evangelism as making connections between the saving events of the death and Resurrection of Christ, personal faith, and God's work for justice and wholeness now. To be converted to Christ is to meet and be known by the God of justice. To meet with injustice, and do something about it, is an encounter with Christ, whether Christ is recognized or not. Evangelism makes those connections explicit.

To those with personal faith and no concern for social justice, evangelism is the good news of the Kingdom. It aims to connect personal faith with the God of justice who gives bread to the hungry, and liberation to the oppressed. To those who work to feed and clothe and visit the Christ who is hungry, naked or imprisoned, but who neither recognize nor know the God of justice, evangelism is the good news of personal salvation.

In the central act of Christian worship, bread and wine, gifts of God, fruit of the earth, work of human hands, become our spiritual food. Without the words of remembrance which connect the bread and wine with the dying and rising of Christ, there is no spiritual food. But if there are only words of remembrance, and no bread, no wine, there is no spiritual food either. The bread of the eucharist is not simply bread for the hungry, it is the bread of life. The cup of wine is the wine of celebration and also the wine of the eternal Kingdom. In the eucharist, word and sacrament belong together, a constant reminder at the heart of Christian worship of the essential unity of personal faith, social justice, and evangelism. To eat the bread of the eucharist without caring for the hungry, to drink the wine without celebrating the goodness and beauty that are in God's world, is, in St Paul's strong words, to eat and drink 'condemnation'.[21]

THE WEEPING PRINCESS

Leo Tolstoy tells the story of a princess who goes to the theatre, driven there in her coach by her old and faithful coachman. The tragedy on stage moves her to tears. Meanwhile outside the night is bitterly cold and a real tragedy takes place. Her faithful coachman, waiting to take her home, freezes to death.

Tolstoy intended the story to buttress arguments he advanced in his later life about the moral value of art. He intended it as a dreadful example of the failure to make connections between art and good behaviour; but all his passionate arguments failed. They proved less telling than the story of the weeping princess and the freezing coachman, which showed only too clearly that art can be wholly impotent. In his earlier life, Tolstoy was strenuously opposed to the idea that art, particularly novels, could be useful, in the sense of 'establishing the correct point of view on social problems'. Its true purpose, he maintained, was 'to make people love life in all its countless, inexhaustible manifestations'; a position he later, sadly, abandoned.[22]

Kenneth Clark, whose personal view of civilization was so cultured and compelling, grew up to love and trust paintings more than people. His son tells that 'he found that art could give him tenderness and solace and energy and tranquillity and beauty without asking for anything in return'.[23] Human beings he found more problematic. His wife, crushed by the casual nature of his many transient relationships, found solace not in art but in alcohol. The irony is greater even than in Tolstoy's fiction – Lord Clark on television eloquently extolling the glories of civilization and art, while at home his wife drank herself into uncivilized oblivion.

There is an important parallel and a major difference between art and worship. The parallel is that art, like worship, is useless, in the strict sense of the word. It has no immediate, practical value. Singing hymns does not feed the hungry, listening to Beethoven does not house the homeless. But worship, like art, has a deep, essential uselessness. It is concerned with ultimate ends, with what human life is really about. Art which degenerates into propaganda, worship which has to be useful in some practical way, misses the point. Art, like worship, takes us out of ourselves. It is a living experience, as profound as that which T. S. Eliot describes when he writes of

> music heard so deeply
> that it is not heard at all,
> but you are the music
> while the music lasts.[24]

An invitation to worship is an invitation to lose ourselves in the life and the love and the contemplation of God. It is the contemplation of God which makes worship different from the experience of even the greatest art. If the princess had been weeping inside a church during an act of worship while her coachman froze outside, the prophet Amos would have had a few crisp things to say to her (Amos 5:21-4). And if Lord Clark had been extolling the importance of worship while his wife suffered, Isaiah would have silenced him (Isaiah 58). For art invites us to see things as they truly are. It may illumine the world, take us out of ourselves, and show us what might be. Worship at its best does all this, but more: it is an encounter with God and therefore an invitation to glimpse the reality and the values of eternity. Art, like worship, beckons; but where art shows us a reflection of life, worship shows us life in the light of God.

THE ART OF TRUE WORSHIP

Art may have a profound effect on people, and it may not. Worship must have a profound effect, or it is not worship. It is not possible to meet with the God of justice and care nothing about injustice. It is not possible to be open to the love of God, and remain indifferent to other people. To care nothing for justice, and to remain unloved and unloving, only indicates that there has been no meeting with God.

Worship changes the way we see the world, it reorders our priorities, it leads us to part company with the easy assumptions of the culture of contentment. Perhaps it was with reference to the power of worship to transform human life that Michael Ramsey once made a remark which sets even the most mundane of worship in a new context: 'Every act of worship', he said, 'is a profound act of service to the whole human race.'[25]

The Sunday morning service in an inner-city Anglican church was following its normal course, a eucharist from the Alternative Service Book; but there was a heavy atmosphere. It was two days after the results of a General Election. Many people in the church, white and black, were profoundly disappointed by the results of the election. Some were not. The service reached the intercessions. The person leading prayed, albeit in a halfhearted way, for the new government – but it was too much. Someone shouted out in disappointment and anger and burst into tears. Others joined in. The liturgy came to a stop, but the real service, the act of worship went on, as people expressed their hurt and bitterness and loss of hope. No-one attempted a quick spiritual solution. They went on to share the bread and the wine, stunned but pleased by what they had done. There was a new reality in the service. They were no longer downcast individuals but a worshipping community who could look each other in the eye. Their act of worship had begun to transform the way they looked at God, at one another, and the world.

ONE WAY FORWARD

In his study of history, Arnold Toynbee suggests that there are four possible ways of looking at life when civilization declines. Three are dead ends: 'Only one, illustrated by the light of Christianity, leads right on.'[26] The three dead ends he calls archaism, futurism and detachment. We have met all three in the course of this study, because they are ways of coping with injustice and every other kind of problem.

Archaism is the attempt to reconstruct in the present a past age made golden by imagination and selective memory. Futurism imagines the bright dawn of a new age and attempts to live in that distant future. Both are attempts to escape, in different directions, from the uncertainty and instability of the present, though archaism is always more popular. 'While it is all too human to seek refuge from a disagreeable present by retreating into a familiar past, human nature is prone to cling to a disagreeable present rather than strike out into an unknown future.'[27]

Detachment is not the practice of silence, solitude and asceticism which enables a person to see the present more clearly. It is, in Toynbee's analysis, another form of escape, this time into a private world. It is what C. P. Snow once described as 'the state of siege', a retreat from the problems by drawing the curtains and settling as comfortably as possible into a private life.[28] The only road which leads on is the way of transformation; but because it is 'illustrated by the life of Christianity', Toynbee chooses to call it 'transfiguration'. It brings us back to the Mount of Transfiguration, from which the journey to the Cross began.

Transfiguration begins by accepting the reality of the situation as it is; and then lifts it into a higher, larger context which gives it clearer perspective, and so provides new direction and fresh resources. This is the movement in which the members of that inner-city church were engaged in their act of worship: rejecting the various forms of escape, they said what they felt about what had happened and began to accept it in the context of worship, a larger, higher context which provided clearer perspective, and enabled them to receive the bread and the wine as signs of that reality which now is, but which may yet be transfigured into the life of the Kingdom of God.

Jesus himself, on the Mount of Transfiguration, accepts the reality of the Cross. 'Two men talked with him, Moses and Elijah, who appeared in glory and spoke of his death' (Luke 9:30-1). Jesus rejects the various ways of escape, a return to the safety of a ministry of preaching and healing, an immediate ascension from the Mount into the glory of heaven, or a retreat into safety in one of the three shelters Peter proposed building. Instead, Jesus sees his coming death, in all its dark and awful reality, in the higher, larger context of the glory of God. In that glory, he is transfigured, and so is able to come down the mountain and begin the journey to Jerusalem and to Calvary.

FROM GLORY TO GLORY

It is a strange and dreadful coincidence that the day on which parts of the Christian Church celebrate the Festival of the Transfiguration, the sixth of August, is also the day on which the first atomic bomb was dropped on Hiroshima – 6 August 1945.

The coincidence does not end with the date. There are the obvious but striking physical similarities, the light, the sound, the cloud. The eye witnesses tell us that the explosion over Hiroshima was like 'the light of many suns'; and that when Jesus was transfigured, 'his face shone like the sun and his clothes became white as the light'. There was a great sound, 'a huge boom like the rumbling of distant thunder'; and a 'voice from heaven, and at the sound of the voice, the disciples fell to the ground in terror'. There was 'an enormous mass of clouds which spread and climbed rapidly into the sky. Then its summit broke open and hung over horizontally'; and while Peter was speaking, 'a bright cloud suddenly overshadowed them.'[29]

More significant than the physical similarities is the fact that the people who experienced these events all knew that they were in the presence of great and awesome power. They were aware that there was great potential for glory and for destruction. Some of the scientists who worked feverishly on nuclear physics in the twenty years before 1945 knew that they were in the presence of the God who had created a world in which such awesome power might be used by human beings.

The man described as the Father of the Bomb, Robert Oppenheimer, was clinging to one of the uprights in the control room when the first bomb was tested in July 1945. A passage from the Bhagavad Gita flashed into his mind: 'If the radiance of a thousand suns were to burst into the sky that would be like the splendour of the Mighty One'. Yet when the sinister cloud rose up, he was reminded of another line from the same writings – 'I am become death, the shatterer of worlds'.

Would it have been better if nuclear power had never been discovered, if we could escape into an earlier, non-nuclear world? One of the Americans in charge of the experiment seemed to think so. He said: 'the strong, sustained awesome roar warned of Doomsday, and made us feel that we puny things were blasphemous to dare tamper with the forces reserved to the Almighty'. Yet Christian faith, when it is true to itself, always takes the bold course of encouraging the search for new knowledge, in the belief that the whole created order reflects the glory of God; that the more we know of the forces of nature, the greater the opportunity to worship and serve God.

Leonard Cheshire, one of the observers who flew above Nagasaki, saw the bomb two weeks earlier. It was being prepared in a Nissen hut and lay on the floor, the size of a football. 'I touched it. Hitherto, the bomb had conjured images of devastating power, unimaginable power, interwoven with an uncomfortable sensation of having to live with something dangerous and volatile that we could not be sure of controlling. But now I had seen it cut down to size. To look at and feel, it was just another metallic object, fashioned by the hand of man, totally subservient to man's will.'[30]

That metallic object symbolizes the power which is available to us, power to do justice or injustice. The amazing combination of knowledge, technological skill, imagination and teamwork which resulted in the bomb led to that most ambiguous of happenings: the destruction of Hiroshima and Nagasaki and the death of many thousands of people; the end of the war and the rescuing of thousands of other people who were close to death; and the beginning of the nuclear age.

TRANSFIGURED BY LOVE

The Gospel of Transfiguration tells that knowledge, power, circumstances and people can be transfigured so that they reflect the glory of God. It was the belief that in the end, the glory of God would be seen, which led Jesus down from the Mountain of the Transfiguration and on to the Way of the Cross. 'Did I not say to you', Jesus told his friends, 'that if you would believe, you would see the Glory of God.' At the moment of betrayal, Jesus said, 'now is the Son of Man glorified, and God is glorified in him'.[31] The betrayal, the arrest, the trial and the Crucifixion are events in which there is grievous injustice and great evil. They are transfigured by love.

'Now is my soul troubled', said Jesus, 'and what shall I say? Father, save me from this hour. But for this cause I came to this hour. Father, glorify your name.' Then came a voice out of heaven saying, 'I have glorified it and will glorify it again.'[32] The choice between justice and injustice, between the light of God's glory and the blinding flash of devastation, between the voice from heaven and the rumble of destruction, between the cloud of God's presence and the cloud of annihilation, is most powerfully expressed in those two famous verses from Little Gidding, written just a few years before Hiroshima:

The Dove descending breaks the air
with flame of incandescent terror
of which the tongues declare
the one discharge from sin and error.
The only hope, or else despair,
lies in the choice of pyre or pyre
to be redeemed from fire by fire.

Who then devised the torment? Love.
Love is the unfamiliar name
behind the hand that wove

the intolerable shirt of flame
which human power cannot remove.
We only live only suspire
Consumed by either fire or fire.[33]

Some parts of the Christian Church use this prayer on the Festival of the Transfiguration, a prayer equally appropriate to Lent, and to the struggle for justice:

Almighty Father,
whose son was revealed in majesty
before he suffered death upon the Cross:
Give us faith to behold his glory,
that we may be strengthened to suffer with him
And be changed into his likeness
from glory to glory,
who is alive and reigns with you
and the Holy Spirit
One God
Now and for ever.

NOTES

NOTES TO CHAPTER 1

1. *Ethics*, p. 179, Aristotle, Parchment Press c4BCE, Penguin Classics 1955.
2. Aristotle p. 172.
3. Aristotle p. 178.
4. Any book concerned with so large a subject as justice is bound to leave out more than can be included; but the decision to leave out two major areas of discussion has been made easier because there are such excellent books on prayer and education. Justice and prayer is the subject of Charles Elliott's *Praying the Kingdom* (Darton, Longman & Todd 1985) while Kenneth Leech provides 'Spiritual resources for the pursuit of justice' in *The Eye of the Storm* (DLT 1992) and Janet Morley has edited a collection of prayers – *Bread of Tomorrow:* Praying with the world's poor (SPCK/ Christian Aid 1992). A revised edition of Brian Wren's *Education for Justice* was published in 1986 (SCM 1977).
5. *Good for the Poor: Christian Ethics and World Development,* p. 51, Michael Taylor, Mowbray 1990. Also *Bad Samaritans: First World Ethics and Third*

World Debt, Paul Vallely, Hodder 1990.

6. Quoted in *No Full Stops in India,* p. 9, Mark Tully, Penguin 1990.
7. *The Future of Man*, p. 100, P. B. Medawar, Shenval 1960.
8. *Darwin,* p. 479, Adrian Desmond & James Moore, Michael Joseph 1991.
9. *Documents of Vatican II: Pastoral Constitution on the Church in the Modern World,* G. Chapman 1967.
10. Aristotle, p. 178.
11. *The Politics,* p. 415, Aristotle, Penguin 1962.
12. *Ethics*, p. 278.
13. Quoted in Dennis (see 18 below).
14. *A Theory of Justice*, p. 4, John Rawls, Oxford 1972.
15. Rawls, section 77.
16. Matthew 16:13-23.
17. *The Foolishness of God*, p. 406, John A. Baker, Darton, Longman & Todd 1970.
18. A detailed study of the Homily is in 'Man beyond Price: Gregory of Nyssa and Slavery', T. J. Dennis in *Heaven and Earth* ed. A. Linzey & P. Wexler, Churchman 1986.
19. *William Wilberforce*, Robert Furneaux, Hamish Hamilton 1974.
20. *Contending Ideologies in South Africa*, p. 70, Ed Leatt, Eerdmans 1986.
21. *I know why the caged bird sings*, p. 131, Maya Angelou, Virago 1984.
22. *Sleeping on a Wire: Conversations with Palestinians in Israel*, pp. 32-3, David Grossman, Jonathan Cape 1993.
23. Grossman, p. 44.

24. Grossman, p. 33.
25. Quoted in the *New Dictionary of Christian Ethics:* article on Equality, Ronald Preston, Ed Macquarrie & Childress, SCM 1967.
26. *The Dark Eye in Africa*, p. 90. Laurens van der Post, Hogarth 1955.
27. *After Virtue*, pp. 252-3, Alasdair Macintyre, Duckworth 1981.
28. Foreword to *Night*, François Mauriac, Penguin 1981.
29. *Sharing a Vision*, p. xii, George Carey, Darton, Longman & Todd 1993.
30. *The Guardian,* 6 July 1989.

NOTES TO CHAPTER 2

1. This comment, and the story in the previous paragraph, are from an unpublished lecture.
2. *The Wisdom of Fools*, p. 43, Mary Grey, SPCK 1993.
3. *Feminist Interpretation of the Bible*, p. 63, Ed. Letty Russell, Blackwell 1985.
4. Paradise Illustrated, A Sequence, *Collected Poems* p. 189, D. J. Enright, Oxford 1987.
5. *A Map of the New Country: Women and Christianity*, p. 8, Sara Maitland, Routledge & Kegan Paul 1983.
6. I owe this vivid picture to Jane Williams who used it in her lectures on spirituality at Salisbury and Wells College.
7. *Paradise Lost* IV 299.635, John Milton.
8. The full text is in *Making Sense*, p. 150-2, John Habgood, SPCK 1993.

9. *Social Justice in the Ancient Near East and the People of the Bible*, Leon Epsztein, SCM 1986.
10. *The Gift of Asher Lev*, p. 333, Chaim Potock, Penguin 1992.
11. *A Grief Observed*, pp. 9-10, C. S. Lewis, Faber 1961.
12. Genesis 26:1-6.
13. *Bible Lives*, pp. 23-32, Jonathan Magonet, SCM 1992.
14. *Moral Man and Immoral Society*, p. 258, Reinhold Niebuhr, SCM 1963.
15. Niebuhr, p. 257.
16. From the Service of Holy Communion in the Book of Common Prayer.
17. Niebuhr, p. 258.
18. *The Foolishness of God*, p. 406.

NOTES TO CHAPTER 3

1. *Moments of Grace*, p. 44, Elizabeth Jennings, Carcanet 1979.
2. *Ethics*, p. 173, Penguin 1955.
3. Romans 12:8.
4. *Church and Nation*, p. 134, William Temple, Macmillan 1915.
5. The Sermon is the seventh homily, on 1 John 4:4-12, *Augustine: Later Works*, p. 312-19, SCM 1955.
6. The information and the quotations relating to these various cases are taken from contemporary records.
7. *A Question of Life*, p. ix, Introduction by Mary Warnock, Blackwell 1985.
8. *Observer* article 29 October 1989.

9. *Utilitarianism and Other Essays*, p. 278, J. S. Mill, Penguin 1987.
10. *Situation Ethics*, p. 33, Joseph Fletcher, SCM 1966.
11. *Honest to God* chapter 6, John Robinson, SCM 1963.
12. *Honest to God*, p. 118.
13. Mark 2:23-8.
14. *Towards a Jewish Theology of Liberation*, pp. 14-15, Marc Ellis, SCM 1987. Also *Beyond Innocence and Redemption: Confronting the Holocaust and Israeli Power*, HarperCollins 1990.
15. *Dimensions of the Holocaust*, p. 12. Lectures at Northwestern University 1977. Also *The Holocaust*, Martin Gilbert, Fontana 1987.
16. *Dimensions*, p. 17.
17. Marc Ellis, p. 23.
18. *The Faith and Doubt of Holocaust Survivors*, p. 215, R. R. Brenner, Free Press (Macmillan) 1980.
19. Brenner, p. 102.
20. Brenner, p. 103.
21. Brenner, p. 108.
22. Brenner, p. 111.
23. *Night*, p. 45, Elie Wiesel, Penguin 1981.
24. *The Times* in an article dicussing the film *Schindler's List*, 19 February 1994.
25. *The Crucified God*, p. 273, Jurgen Moltmann, SCM 1974.
26. *The Trial of God: the scene*, Elie Wiesel, Shocken 1979.
27. *The Trial of God*, p. 125.
28. *Night*, pp. 76-7.
29. Mark 15:33–7.
30. *The Koran* 4:158, p. 77, Penguin Classics 1956. A

penetrating discussion of the sovereignty of God in Islam and in Christianity is in *Sandals at the Mosque*, Kenneth Cragg, SCM 1959.

31. *Night*, pp. 10-11.

NOTES TO CHAPTER 4

1. The full text of all the resolutions is in *After the Storm: Lessons from the Gulf War*, Ed. J. Nye and R. K. Smith, Madison Books 1992.
2. Quoted in *After the Storm*.
3. *After the Storm*, p. 210.
4. 'St Augustine's views on War', pp. 1-15, R. A. Markus in *The Church and War*, Blackwell 1983.
5. *Towards a Jewish Theology of Liberation*, p. 93, Marc Ellis, SCM 1987.
6. *Changing Britain: social diversity and moral unity*, p. 1, BSR 1987.
7. *Church and Nation in a Secular Age*, p. 168, John Habgood, Darton, Longman & Todd 1983.
8. *Christianity and Social Order*, p. 97, William Temple, Penguin 1942, Shepheard-Walwyn 1976.
9. Temple, p. 97.
10. Temple, p. 29.
11. There are discussions of what is sometimes called the 'middle axiom' approach in *William Temple and Christian Social Ethics Today*, Alan Suggate, T. & T. Clark 1987; and in *Beliefs, Values and Policies: Conviction politics in a secular age*, Duncan Forrester, Oxford 1989.
12. Quoted in *From Boom to Bust*, p. 64, David Smith, Penguin 1992.

13. *Utilitarianism*, p. 288, J. S. Mill, Penguin Classics 1987.
14. Mill, pp. 288-9.
15. John 18:14.
16. Mill, p. 337.
17. *Young India*, 8.1.1925: in *All Men are Brothers*, Continuum 1980.
18. *After Virtue*, p. 69.
19. *Making Sense*, pp. 95–109, John Habgood, SPCK 1993.
20. *The Affluent Society,* pp. 87-8 from chapter 7, 'Inequality', J. K. Galbraith, Penguin 1958.
21. *Popular Writings*, p. 325, Reimer 1911.
22. *A Theory of Justice*, chapter 3, John Rawls, Oxford 1972.
23. *Anarchy, State and Utopia,* Robert Nozick, Basic Books, New York 1974.
24. *The Independent,* 11 October 1993.
25. *The Culture of Contentment*, p. 27, J. K. Galbraith, Penguin 1993.
26. *The Politics*, 1257b41 p. 85, Penguin 1962.
27. Genesis 23.
28. *We Belong to the Land*, pp. 2-3, Elias Chacour and Mary Jensen, Marshall Pickering 1992.
29. *Pax Romana and the Peace of Christ*, p. 62, Klaus Wengst, SCM. 1987.
30. *Justice and only Justice*, p. 187, Naim A'teek, Orbis 1989. Also *Introducing Liberation Theology*, L. & C. Boff, Orbis 1987. *A Theology of Liberation*, G. Gutierrez, SCM 1974.

NOTES TO CHAPTER 5

1. Matthew 27:20-26.
2. *Psychology, The Science of Mind and Behaviour,* chapter 12, Richard D. Gross, Hodder 1987.
3. Gross, p. 320 quoted from *Obedience to Authority,* S. Milgram, Harper and Row, 1974.
4. The research was done by a professor at the Hebrew University in Jerusalem. The figures were provided for me by Dennis Madden, Lecturer in Peace Studies at the Tantur Institute.
5. *The Culture of Contentment,* J. K. Galbraith, Penguin 1992.
6. Galbraith, p. 26.
7. *After Virtue*, p. 263, Alasdair Macintyre, Duckworth, Second edition 1985.
8. *The Victorian Church*, Volume 1 p. 351, Owen Chadwick, A. & C. Black 1970.
9. Debate at the Edinburgh Science Festival, 1992.
10. *The Persistence of Faith*, p. 93, Jonathan Sacks, Weidenfeld & Nicholson 1992.
11. Sacks, p. 94.
12. The complete text of the speech is published in *Christianity and Politics,* Hugh Montefiore, Macmillan 1990.
13. *Religion and the Rise of Capitalism,* p. 192, R. H. Tawney, 1926, Penguin 1961.
14. The quotation was used by Sir Patrick Hastings in his cross-examination of Laski during a libel trial: in *Sir Patrick Hastings: His Life and Cases,* H. Montgomery Hyde, Hamish Hamilton 1960.
15. *Miracles,* p. 194, C. S. Lewis, Bles 1947.
16. There is a passionate discussion of these questions

in *Suffering*, Dorothy Soelle, Fortress Press, 1975.
17. *We Drink from our own Wells*, p. 117, G. Gutierrez, Orbis 1984.
18. Gutierrez, p. 118.
19. Gutierrez, p. 116.
20. Quoted in *The Missionary Factor in East Africa*, p. 276, R. Oliver, Longmans 1952.
21. 1 Corinthians 11:29.
22. *Tolstoy: a biography*, pp. 267-8, A. N. Wilson, Penguin 1989.
23. The quotation is taken from a television portrait of Lord Clark, BBC2 1993.
24. 'The Dry Salvages' from *The Four Quartets*, p. 33, T. S. Eliot, Faber 1944.
25. He made this comment in answer to a question, though it is probably included somewhere in his writings.
26. *A Study of History*, p. 530, Arnold Toynbee, Abridged version Oxford 1947.
27. Toynbee, p. 515.
28. *The State of Siege,* C. P. Snow, Oxford 1970.
29. The description is that of a Japanese professor who witnessed it from three miles away: in *Death in Life*, R. J. Lifton, Weidenfeld & Nicholson 1967.
30. *The Light of Many Suns*, pp. 25-6, L. Cheshire, Methuen 1985.
31. John 13:31-2: also John 17.
32. John 12:27-8.
33. *The Four Quartets*, p. 42, T. S. Eliot, Faber 1944.

Fount Classics

AUTOBIOGRAPHY OF A SAINT

St Thérèse of Lisieux

Translated by Ronald Knox

St Thérèse of Lisieux, known as the 'Little Flower', who died in 1897 virtually unknown outside her convent, is now recognized as the most popular and influential saint of our times. She was canonized in 1925, and successive Popes have recommended her as an authoritative spiritual guide for the twentieth century and beyond.

The immense popularity of Thérèse is largely based upon this book. It is her own personal testimony. Written at odd moments in school exercise books and on scraps of paper, it gives a vivid human account of the life of a saint from the inside; intimate, spontaneous and sparkling throughout with a delightful humour.

Ronald Knox was a witty and brilliant Anglican priest and scholar who became one of this century's most famous converts to Roman Catholicism, and went on in the 1940s to make one of the greatest modern translations of the Bible.

Fount Classics

THE PILGRIM'S PROGRESS

John Bunyan

Written in prison, where Bunyan had been sent for unauthorized preaching, and first published in 1967, this classic story has been described as the most popular work of Christian spirituality written in English, and as the first English novel. It describes the road to the Celestial City, by way of Doubting Castle, the Delectable Mountains, Vanity Fair and other places whose names have entered the very fabric of the language.

Fascinating as literature, entertaining as story, profound as spiritual teaching for the soul's journey, *The Pilgrim's Progress* is 'a masterpiece which generation after generation of ordinary men and women have taken to their hearts'.

HUGH ROSS WILLIAMSON

Fount Classics
BIOGRAPHY

JOHN BUNYAN
The Christian
Gordon Wakefield

John Bunyan, born in 16628 son of a Bedford tinker, and teenage soldier in the army of Robert Cromwell, fell into a kind of religious madness and emerged from this a soldier in the army of Christ: a fiery preacher in the radical Puritan tradition. His fervour brought him into conflict with the Restoration government, and he spent much time in prison. It was there he wrote his famous masterpiece, *The Pilgrim's Progress.*

This outstanding biography takes Bunyan seriously as a spiritual guide, and sets his life in the context of English Christianity, as well as the political conflicts of his time.

Gordon Wakefield was Principal of the Queen's College Birmingham from 1979 until his retirement in 1987. He is a Methodist minister and director of the Alister Hardy Centre for Research into Religious Experience. He was the first Methodist minister to be awarded the Lambeth doctorate of divinity. He lives in Lichfield.

'Wakefield's excellent book helps us to understand why Bunyan's influence continues down the centuries and across the continents.' *Baptist Times*

'The chief merit of this impressive theological life is to bring back a Bunyan with a vibrant word for now, one that leaps all denominational frontiers.' *Methodist Recorder*

Fount Classics
BIOGRAPHY

IGNATIUS LOYOLA

Philip Caraman

St Ignatius, founder of the Jesuits or Society of Jesus, was born in 1491, the year before the discovery of the New World by Columbus. He grew up in a golden age of the Spanish court, himself a courtier, a knight, a gambler and a ladies' man.

Wounded in defending the citadel of Pamplona, he underwent a dramatic conversion and became a leading figure in the Counter-Reformation. A man of wit and humanity, of enormous energy and administrative ability, he was also one of the greatest of mystics, and in struggling against his own failures and shortcomings became one of the great influences on world history.

Philip Caraman is a member of the Society of Jesus and a historian of world renown. His previous books include *The Lost Paradise,* the story of the Jesuit Reductions in Paraguay and the subject of the film *The Mission,* and the international bestseller *John Gerard*.

'A brilliant and beautiful achievement'
ELIZABETH LONGFORD

'A vivid and veracious biography which all can enjoy for its human and historical interest.'
A. L. ROWSE

Fount Classics
SPIRITUAL DIRECTION

FINDING GOD IN ALL THINGS

The Way of St Ignatius

Margaret Hebblethwaite

St Ignatius of Loyola, the sixteenth-century founder of the Jesuits, left behind him a living tradition of prayer in his Spiritual Exercises. Over the centuries these have been enormously influential; today there is more interest than ever in Ignatian spirituality, among ordinary people as well as religious professionals, and across all the Christian denominations.

In this book Margaret Hebblethwaite interprets the ideas of Ignatius for the present day. She combines sound practical advice on how to set about praying with an understanding of the deep mystery and beauty of prayer; prayer which can lead us, not to leave the world behind, but to make full use of all our God-given opportunities so that we too can learn to find God in all things.

Margaret Hebblethwaite was born in 1951, studied at Oxford and at the Gregorian University in Rome. She is a founder member and former committee member of the Catholic Theological Association of Great Britain. Her books include *Motherhood and God* and the recently published *Basic is Beautiful.* She is now assistant editor of the Catholic weekly *The Tablet.*

Fount Classics
BIOGRAPHY

JOHN XXIII
Pope of the Council
Peter Hebblethwaite

Born into a simple family on the northern edge of Italy, Angelo Giuseppe Roncalli spent much of his working life in unfashionable diplomatic postings in Sofia and Istanbul until his surprise appointment as Papal Representative in Paris in the difficult years immediately after the Second World War. In 1953 he became Patriarch of Venice in what was assumed to be the last appointment of a man whom many considered worthy but naïve. When at the age of 77 he was elected to succeed the austere and aristocratic Pope Pius XII they called him the stop-gap Pope, not expected to reign long or to do much. Yet, in a mere four and a half years Pope John XXIII transformed the Roman Catholic Church.

He called the Second Vatican Council and gave it a vision for the future. He mediated in the Cuban missile crisis and promoted dialogue between Kennedy and Kruschev. With his encyclical *Pacem in Terris*, he made hope seem impossible again.

Peter Hebblethwaite's definitive biography, first published in 1984, was a landmark of ecclesiastic history. It is here reissued with a new introduction in paperback format.

Fount Classics
BIOGRAPHY

PAUL VI
The First Modern Pope
Peter Hebblethwaite

Peter Hebblethwaite, almost certainly the leading Vatican historian and commentator to be writing in English today, has written the essential biography of Paul VI, who was Pope from 11963 to 1978. The book has been several years in the writing, and draws radical new conclusions about Paul's contribution to the modern papacy. Unlike his predecessor, John XXIII, there are few anecdotes about Paul. There is consequently no 'industry' surrounding him. And yet, Hebblethwaite argues, he was probably a richer and deeper personality, and his pontificate was of more decisive importance for the future of the Church. There had, he suggests, been unreasonable liberal optimism at the death of John XXIII. Paul was bound to disappoint, given these expectations. As it was, he consolidated the post-Vatican II Church with a mixture of openness and fidelity. Peter Hebblethwaite's book is a classic of its kind, glittering with detail and informed comment.

An ex-Jesuit priest who went to Rome to report on the final session of the Second Vatican Council, Peter Hebblethwaite now lives in Oxford and is a freelance writer. He has written many books including a much celebrated biography of Pope John XXIII, which accompanies this book as a paperback.